LARSON
DUKE OF MONGOLIA

BY

FRANS AUGUST LARSON

With Illustrations

BOSTON

LITTLE, BROWN, AND COMPANY

1930

THE ATLANTIC MONTHLY PRESS BOOKS
ARE PUBLISHED BY
LITTLE, BROWN, AND COMPANY
IN ASSOCIATION WITH
THE ATLANTIC MONTHLY COMPANY

FRANS AUGUST LARSON

DUKE OF MONGOLIA

My deepest gratitude is due to
Nora Waln
for collaboration in the compiling
and the writing of this book

CONTENTS

ILLUSTRATIONS

LARSON, DUKE OF MONGOLIA

I

THE NOBLES

I CAME out to Mongolia from Sweden in 1893, for the
Christian Missionary Alliance of New York, and
worked under their direction until 1900. I was
twenty-three years old. Except for six weeks spent
in England, this was my first venture away from my
homeland. I settled first at Paotow, on the China
border of Mongolia. Here I began to study the Mongolian language. I could find no books from which
to work, but I secured a teacher, and used the method
of asking him the name of this thing and the name
of that — in this way making up a vocabulary. This
was not very satisfactory. I made slow progress. I
wished I might learn by living where Mongol was
the native tongue, but it was not easy to secure
residence within Mongolia.

The Mongols are a proud people and do not en-
courage foreigners to settle among them.

I was attracted by what I saw of Mongolia across
the border. All my life I had liked horses. I grew up
with horses in Sweden. I groomed, fed, and rode
them from my earliest boyhood. I longed to talk and
live with these people who galloped through the
streets of Paotow. I admired their free, easy grace and
the jolly good nature with which they seemed to
joke with each other.

I was very homesick in those days. The Mongols seemed more akin to me than any other folk near.

The whole of Mongolia then was divided into innumerable states each ruled over by a nobleman, with the power of an absolute monarch in his own territory. All these noblemen traced their right to rule back to the old days of Genghis Khan; many of them were direct descendants of Genghis's sons.

My opportunity to enter Mongolia finally came through the courtesy of the monarch of Ordos, the state whose borders touched Paotow. I made friends first with the Chinese military official in Paotow, through his horses, and he took me with him one day when he went to call on the Prince of Ordos. Later the Prince told the Manchu official to fetch me to the wedding festivities of his son, the Duke of Ordos.

These festivities lasted for three days. The Prince and his family were all very kind to me. I was very happy during the visit and very sorry when the end of the third day came and the mandarin took me up to bid the Prince farewell.

The Prince of Ordos spoke to me kindly. I knew enough Mongolian by then to understand that he asked me to stay longer. I stayed.

Living quarters were prepared for me inside the monarch's residence. He selected, personally, a teacher to help me with the language. I had daily lessons, but more helpful than these lessons was the opportunity of hearing Mongolian spoken all day long. I had to speak Mongol too, because there was no other means by which I could let my thoughts be known to the people around me.

The Prince gave me good horses to ride and took me out with him continually on trips over the state. The Prince's wife visited me daily, always bringing one or two of the ladies in waiting with her to my quarters. She became my mother adviser in the small but important details of Mongolian etiquette.

One day she brought a crowd of young ladies to visit me. They soon let me know that they had come for the special purpose of examining my knees. A Chinese trader who had come to the Palace to sell silk brocades had told them that a foreigner's knees could not be moved in the same way as those of the Mongols or the Chinese. I was embarrassed, but she was the wife of the absolute ruler of the state as well as my hostess. She repeated her request, and I uncovered my knees. Then she and her ladies in waiting pinched and pushed them backwards and forwards. Finally they expressed their opinion that my legs were made in the same way as theirs. So they were satisfied, and I could cover my knees again.

Another day the ruler's wife appeared saying that she thought it was very bad for a young man to live without a wife. She considered it too lonely for me, and that I should learn the language very much quicker if I had a woman to talk to always. She said that since I was an orphan with no parents to arrange a marriage for me, and in reality in Ordos in the position of the Prince's son, she had chosen a nice girl from her ladies in waiting. She told me that all arrangements for the marriage had been made. She said the girl was beautiful, high-spirited, and an excellent horsewoman — and in love with me. She was both surprised and annoyed when I declined her good offer. The Prince laughed heartily when he heard of it.

I lived under the patronage of the monarch of Ordos for three months, and then, with introductions from him, I went north to Urga to enjoy the experience of life in the capital of Mongolia, where many nobles were gathered, as well as the advantages of a cosmopolitan language.

In Urga people were very kind to me and exceedingly hospitable as the Prince of Ordos had been. Here I made friends who have remained my friends all my life. All the monarchs of the states of North Mongolia had royal tents pitched in Urga. Some of them, in addition to governing their own states, had duties relating to Mongolia as a whole. There were also many nobles who came up for a few months every year to be near the Living Buddha, who was, in addition to being the Mongol God, a very popular man.

In Urga I made friendships which opened the door into every state in Mongolia later. I did not consciously do this, for I was a thoughtless, rollicking lad in those days, keen on hunting parties and sports of all kinds. The young Mongols of my own age were good companions, and I was never homesick after I had entered Ordos.

Some years after I first went to Mongolia, and when I had lived in many different parts of the country, I was called up to Urga and created a Mongol duke by the Emperor of Mongolia, with full rights equal to those of a Mongol prince's son. This honor was a tremendous surprise to me.

In Ordos I was taught to conduct myself as a Mongol gentleman, and in addition I learned much concerning life in the country and the method by which each ruler governs his small state. All this has been very useful to me.

Each ruler has his advisers and officials, some of noble birth and some who are from the commoners. Most of them were, and still are, very wealthy, although they have no money in the banks. Their wealth is counted according to the number of horses they own. Many princes possess thousands, in addition to numberless sheep, camels, and cattle. As there are no banks in Mongolia, a nobleman, when he has some money, at once turns it into animals of some kind.

Many of the Mongolian nobles have built stone palaces, elaborate structures patterned ·after the Manchu palaces. But very few of them actually dwell inside of stone walls. They use these palaces on state occasions, at festival times, and whenever they wish to make a great display. The average Mongol is more comfortable in a tent. They have a distrust of the softening influences of luxurious modes of life. I have never met a Mongolian noblewoman who did not consider life inside of walls unhealthy.

Even when a monarch does dwell in his palace, the heir to the throne is brought up in a yurta beyond the palace gates, where he lives exactly the same hardening life that his ancestors have lived for centuries. His food is the simple strengthening food of the commoner — mutton and curd cheese; his drink, mare's milk. He learns to ride as Genghis Khan rode, and to meet wolves, weather, and hunger with a stout heart. A monarch on the Mongolian plateau must be a man of physical prowess who does not know the word "fear."

The ruler of a Mongolian state does not receive an allowance in money with which to meet his needs; but the people of the state must supply him with anything he requires. So although he may possess many thousands of horses, which he has inherited perhaps from his mother, as his own fortune, still when he travels it is the custom for him to use state horses. And when he travels he also draws upon the country for men, tents, food, and anything else that he needs. The people have to provide him all the year round with felt for his tents, saddles, carts, oxen, clothes for himself and family — in fact, anything within reason that he needs.

All royal residences, whether movable yurtas or stone palaces, have connected with them a "yamen," or place where all government business is transacted. Here the nobleman himself may go often, if he pleases, and personally attend to all the affairs of the state; but in actual practice he is much more likely to let this work be done by commoners who are responsible to him.

In the yamen all disputes between individuals within the state are decided, criminals are punished, tributes are determined upon, and official dispatches on outside matters are written. Usually the man in charge of the yamen — or the men, if there happen to be several — talks with the nobleman concerning any important question before they reach a decision. All dispatches must be shown to him before they are sealed.

According to the old common law of Mongolia, still in force to-day, except where Soviet influence has come in in North Mongolia, any and every citizen in a state has the right to personal audience with his ruler; but only in very special cases do citizens take advantage of this right. Usually all troubles are settled peacefully at the yamen. Murder is a crime practically unheard of in Mongolia, and with the exception of Urga the country has no prisons. None are needed. The worst crimes are those sufficiently punished by a spanking administered at the yamen.

Each man and woman in a Mongol state owes one moon of annual service to the ruler of the state if that service is needed. It is the custom to call workers in turn. The man or woman is used for whatever duty he or she is fitted to perform. One woman may be able to mend tents but would be impossible as a lady in waiting; a man might be a good magistrate but out of place as a cook. The Mongols are a people of common sense, and do not make mistakes in delegating a person to a job.

This constant movement of the population to the royal residence and out again into the state has a dual value, for it makes all citizens well acquainted with the ruler. They watch him grow from babyhood to old age. They know him intimately, and he knows each and all of them.

All noblemen in Mongolia are called "black men," to distinguish them from the lamas. This name comes from the fact that they all wear long queues and their hair is black. The lamas' heads are shaven.

A ruler has the right to as many wives as he chooses, provided the women desire to marry him. Every woman in Mongolia is as free as a man, and while a young girl can be forced to fulfill an engagement made for her by her parents, according to common law she has a right to leave the man with whom she has gone through the marriage ceremony three days after the wedding day, whether he be nobleman or commoner.

A ruler has practically unlimited power. This might seem to be a very dangerous thing. In a few cases it is, — that is, when the monarch born happens to be a bad-tempered person, — but on the whole the Mongols are generous, good-tempered people, fun-loving and hospitable and kind.

The occasional vile-dispositioned ruler makes havoc in his state during his reign. His bad example not only makes trouble for himself, but breeds discontent among his subjects. Horses are the most usual source of trouble. An unwise prince covets personal wealth, and as the Mongols have no banks, but hold their fortune in herds, a wicked prince forces his subjects to give him all the best horses for his private herds. He also seizes upon the best wells and the grazing places without thought for the general prosperity of the state. But such men are rare.

I have traveled east and west, north and south, and been entertained by most of the noblemen of Mongolia. In many states I have known the father as monarch, and then his son as monarch, and now know the little boy who is growing up to rule, and in all my experiences I have met with but three men who were not just rulers, with greater thought for the prosperity of their state than for their personal fortune.

It is bred through centuries in the Mongol nobleman to consider it his duty to rule wisely and well for the span of years allotted to him.

North Mongolia, when I first lived there in 1893, and up to 1923, was governed by four khans. These provinces were again subdivided into smaller states, each ruled over by a prince or a duke, usually a close relative to the khan.

This is not so now, because in North Mongolia Soviet ideas and Soviet political advisers control affairs; with their coming all the nobles have disappeared, as they disappeared in Russia. In Eastern, Inner, and Western Mongolia the old system prevails. Here the nobles, from the smallest to the greatest, still live a very independent life, absolute emperors over their own realm.

Chahar, bordering on China, has always been governed from Kalgan during the years that I have lived in Mongolia — first by the Manchus, then by the various heads of government in China since the proclamation of the Chinese republic, in 1911. This part of Mongolia is now under the Nationalist form of government, and is being settled by Chinese farmers, who are driving the Mongols farther and farther back into Inner Mongolia.

China was a vassal of Mongolia for several centuries, but since the seventeenth century, when the great K'ang-hsi sat on the throne of China, Mongolia has been pictured on the map as a vassal country to China. Mongols say that this is because they do not bother to write histories or draw maps. They do not want China, but they helped the Manchus take it, and then made an agreement of allegiance subject to the following conditions: that Mongolia should not be colonized by the Chinese; that no Chinese troops should be stationed in Mongolia; and that the internal organization and customs of Mongolia should not be interfered with.

During my lifetime in China, the professed Mongolian allegiance to the Manchu rulers of China, except for Chahar, has been a mutual-benefit arrangement; the Mongols paid no material tribute to the Manchu Throne as the Chinese were forced to do; rather, many of the Mongolian noblemen received rich gifts for their loyalty.

The Mongol nobles had the right to sit at table with the Manchu Emperor — a right which they stoutly maintained by insisting upon sitting down with him once every year. And instead of the marriage of Manchu women with Mongols being forbidden, as it was with Chinese until 1909, such unions were encouraged. Many reluctant Manchu princesses were sent as brides to the noblemen of the plains, because the Manchu Throne desired to make the rulers of the north cousins in more than mere name. At all festivities in the Forbidden City in Peking, Mongolian noblemen and their wives and daughters were welcomed with honors equal to those accorded to Manchu nobles. The wedding of an emperor was always a time of great festivity, in which the Mongols took an equal part with the Manchus.

Manchu officials were sent to Mongolia ostensibly to control Chinese merchants who came in to trade. Until the time when the Living Buddha was made Emperor a Manchu governor was always resident in Urga, where there was a Chinese merchant population of about eight thousand domiciled in an area assigned to them. Chinese were not permitted to have their wives with them in Mongolia, as their stay was only a visit and the presence of wives would lead to permanent settling. The Manchu officials were mostly too wise to penetrate into Mongolian affairs, and, when they did, it was usually with disastrous results. Few of them ever learned the Mongolian language. Then too, the Manchu was not accustomed to the rough life of the plains, not at home on horseback or in a tent, and so usually limited his place of residence and his travel to Urga or Kalgan or some small border city.

But sometimes the Manchus did have to travel, and during their time in Mongolia the Chinese Government maintained state or government roads for their use, with relay stations of ponies about every twenty miles. I have often traveled with a pass for this road, sometimes in company with Manchu officials, sometimes alone. In addition to the relay of ponies, one was always provided with an escort, sometimes a man and sometimes a woman, who rode along to show the way. In addition to this escort, the pass gave one the right to a sheep, or part of a sheep, at each station for food, with mare's milk and cheese and tea. Often when I have traveled with a Manchu I have seen him demand the value of the mutton in silver at each station, but this action always gave that person a very bad reputation all along the line.

The Mongolian nobleman or woman, or one of their deputies, when in haste, travels by what is called "lasso relay." I once traveled across Inner Mongolia in this fashion. A prince, whose guest I was at the time, supplied me with a pass and started me off from his palace, mounted on one of his best horses, and accompanied by two well-mounted men. One of these men traveled light — that is, without any pack over his saddle — and carried a lasso. The other man had, in a roll behind him, the few necessities I take with me when traveling abroad in Mongolia. We galloped across the rolling green plain until our horses began to show fatigue. Then the man with the lasso dashed up to the first horse herd that we happened to sight and, assisted by their herdsman, lassoed three fresh mounts. We put our horses' saddles on these horses and let our tired animals go free in the stranger herd.

At a gallop we went on in a straight line toward our destination. Again our horses showed fatigue.

We kept our eyes open for the sight of a herd. Again the lasso man and the herdsman of that particular herd lassoed fresh mounts and left our tired ones free to graze. So we went on day after day, the same courtesy being extended to us in neighboring princes' states as we passed.

Afterwards it is customary for the owners of the horses to make the exchange with their neighbors and so regain their property.

When we were hungry, the lasso man would stop at a yurta and explain that I was a friend of the prince, and we would be given food and drink. At the end of every day he would find a yurta where we could sleep, have a sheep killed for the evening meal, and help to drive cows in to be milked if I desired milk.

On the second day my lasso man and his companion said that they were very tired and wished to turn back home. They explained to me that in such a case it was customary to hand over their jobs to other men. This these two did, supplying me with two men who carried out the work faithfully.

I found this a very speedy way to travel, and since I have done it myself I never doubt the Mongol nobleman who tells me that he has ridden the equivalent of one hundred English miles a day. I found that it was not hard to do, as we went at a run all the time, and lost little time in changing horses or in eating or drinking. Continuously riding fresh horses is not tiring.

A Mongolian nobleman and his family out traveling for pleasure only, probably on a visit to a neighboring state ruler, use a large number of horses and servants, but they do not travel very fast. They usually camp by every pretty place and spend long hours feasting and joking, making just as much out of the picnic as possible.

During thirty-five years I have stayed with many Mongolian rulers. From more states than I could count on the fingers of both hands I have continual assurances that if I am ever in need of a home I am welcome there for as long as I wish to come and stay. As a guest in any of these families I have always had an exceedingly good time. They are simple-hearted, healthy folk.

Mongolian nobles as well as commoners enjoy fun and jokes, and have ample leisure in which to enjoy life.

One prince whom I often visit always has his people in to sing and to play the flute for me. He arranges hunting parties and wrestling matches and impromptu theatricals. The women of the Mongolian families are not secluded, but mix as freely as the men with guests in social contact and in the enjoyment of sports.

Princes often take great pains to play a joke on some brother noble. I remember once visiting a duke and seeing two messengers from a neighboring prince come in. They carried a parcel which they offered to my host on the usual Mongolian silk scarf of light blue, — which is the accepted Mongolian visiting card, — and inquired after the duke's health. Kneeling with great ceremony, they handed over the present, saying that it was a very valuable gift from their lord and master.

The duke showed his pleasure. He hastily set to work opening the parcel. He took off one layer after another of wrapping paper. The parcel grew smaller and smaller in size. Each layer of covering was securely tied up with intricate knots of string. These he finally cut with his hunting knife. At last there was only a tiny ball left. As he pulled off the last wrapping the duke exclaimed, "It must be the old carved coral I have so often admired."

But it was only a stone! His face showed the same disappointment that a child's might have shown. He scratched his head in dazed perplexity, then burst into loud laughter. When I left, two weeks later, he was still trying to think up a better joke to play on the prince.

Another noble whom I knew was in love with the sister of a prince, but he did not dare tell her, as she was higher in rank than he. The prince, however, knew about it. One day he sent a message over to the lesser nobleman's state to tell him that on a certain day he would come with his whole family for a visit. The lesser noble set to work to prepare a great feast. His servants were busy from morning until night, as their master desired to give the best entertainment possible to the girl he loved and her family. Everything was ready at last.

The guests arrived. When the first greetings were over, the prince said to the lesser nobleman that he would very much like to see his horse carriage. This carriage was really the most treasured possession of the lesser noble. It had been brought out at great expense from Europe. The nobleman had built a

special little house in his palace yard in which to
keep it. He at once escorted the prince and his sister
to the carriage house, and we all talked for a considerable time about various points of the carriage.

The nobleman and the prince's sister were induced
by the prince to sit in it so that we could see how
the springs worked. Then the prince pulled me by
the sleeve and motioned to me to slip out. We went
quietly through the door. The prince pushed the
padlock shut, and, unheeding the call of his sister,
led me away to the palace. Here he ordered the
servants to lay the feast.

Others of his family asked for his sister. He said
she would be coming back soon. We feasted and
talked for a good long time. Then the prince went
back to the carriage house and unbolted the door.
Laughingly he said to his friend and his own sister,
"I was sure that both of you preferred love to an
ordinary meal."

The poor noble, very red in the face, and much
embarrassed, had no answer to make; but he was
probably very glad the prince had made things so
easy for him. A short time after this he and the
princess were happily married.

It is the custom for the ruler of each state to hold
a big festival every summer, when all his people
flock together and enjoy themselves. On all these
occasions the ruler and his family wear their finest
robes. These festivals last a week or ten days. Horse
races and wrestling matches are held every day.
The best horses of the state are entered in the races.

All the strong young men, lamas and laymen, take part in the wrestling matches. The ruler occupies the chief place and plays the most important part in judging the contest and the matches. In addition to the sports, there are two feasts each day, but probably more important than any other feature of the festivals is the opportunity they give for the nomad people of the plains to enjoy each other's society.

At this time of the year, they who at all other times live in scattered tents wherever the water and the grass happen to be best for their herds come together for the great state merrymaking, and many a marriage is arranged during the festival time.

One of my friends, who, in addition to his residence in the state he governed, had a residence in Urga, was the Prince of Hanta. As I also lived in Urga many years and we had a common love of outdoor life and hunting, he used often to arrange excursions into the mountains beyond Urga for my pleasure.

I remember one trip when we were about twelve men in the party, with a cook and two expert trackers. We left Urga at three o'clock in the morning, a merry party all mounted on good horses, with plenty of extra mounts led along, in addition to pack animals carrying provisions.

The Prince gave me a strong, sure-footed mountain horse of high spirit, and I enjoyed myself immensely. Before noon we crossed into the Prince's own state and were soon in a thick forest of tall trees. We camped for lunch beside a brook of clear water. After food and a short rest we each took a horse and scattered out into the woods to see what we could find, each of us, of course, intending to surprise the rest of the party by returning with a wild boar or a reindeer.

But no one was so fortunate. The only bag of the afternoon was a small mountain deer brought in by one of the noblemen and added to our meat supply. We then put up blue cloth tents for the night, and felled several trees, which we added to a great bonfire of deadwood.

Hungry after our exercise, we sat around the fire and toasted strips of meat on greenwood prongs. We took the edge off our appetites with these titbits while we waited for the special dish that the Prince had ordered his cook to prepare.

A large hole had been dug in the ground and shovels of glowing wood ashes put into it. Meat had been laid on the ashes and then the hole filled up level with more hot ashes. These ashes had been covered with earth, which was heaped up in a great mound. In this hole the meat baked for several hours, and when it was served it was delicious.

After dinner we all told hunting adventures. The Prince, who was an excellent story-teller, recounted the experiences of his early hunting days, when as a young man with no governmental duties he used to live in the mountains for many weeks at a time in company only with an old hunter to whom his father entrusted him. No one used the blue tents. We all dropped off to sleep lying around the fire.

Early next morning our trackers reported that

THE PRINCE OF HAN'TA AND HIS SON-IN-LAW

they had found tracks of four reindeer who must have passed our camp site a day or two earlier. They said that there was one big bull, one cow, a calf, and one three-year-old.. This they knew from the hoof prints.

Our whole party were soon in the saddle. The Prince had to order the cook off his horse, else our tents and equipment would have been left scattered about where they were dropped in the general excitement of every man to be in the chase. I felt sorry for the cook left behind to load the pack horses and go on as best he could. We were all very much excited and rode wildly after the mounted trackers, who tore ahead into the thick forest-covered mountains to the north.

We rode madly that day. Our animals were lathered with sweat and somewhat blown, but kept at work with valiant courage. Toward evening our trackers called out that the hoof prints were now much fresher but that the reindeer might still be a good distance off.

The Prince ordered a halt beside a crystal-clear mountain spring. We tended our horses first — watered them when they had cooled down, and turned them out hobbled to graze on good mountain grass. Then we made a fire, toasted strips of a mountain deer that we had killed a little distance from the spring, and fell asleep to the murmur of swaying tree tops.

The next morning we were again early on the chase, and at noon the trackers were confident that we were approaching near to the reindeer. We kept up our spirits, enlivened by the nearness of our prey. The trackers grew very excited. Finally they halted the entire party. They begged us to make camp and wait while they scouted quietly ahead, lest our noise should spoil the chances of getting the game. The mountain grass was very thick on the slope just at that place. We let our horses feed while we had some lunch.

Toward the evening the trackers returned and reported that the reindeer were feeding quietly behind another mountain not much more than three miles from us. It was decided not to disturb the deer, as the light was fast failing. We made our camp as on the previous night.

Our trackers were out early next morning. They soon came back with word that the animals were very near the same place at which they had seen them the day before. The two men explained to the Prince that there was a small mountain range between us and the reindeer, with a big river running through the valley just below the range. They suggested that we should be stationed at intervals along the mountain range while they drove the reindeer in between the river and the mountain.

We all thought this an excellent idea and scattered out along the ridge of the mountain, from where we could see a fine river splashing through the valley four or five hundred yards below us. We waited for some time. Then the trackers gave a signal that the animals were approaching. I hardly got my eyes on something moving when shots rang out on every side of me. I was among the last to fire my rifle.

The reindeer were not more than five hundred yards from me, or, for that matter, from any of us, but such was our excitement that we banged away thirty or forty shots with repeating rifles and not one of the animals was even hit. They swam across the river and disappeared safely into the forest beyond at a beautiful trot!

The Prince gathered us together and told us that we were a bunch of proper fools. He asked us if no one had ever taught us how to sight a rifle, and whether we had never been told that when lying in a high place, firing at an object below, and hilariously excited, we should aim far under the mark if we hoped to hit it. I have used this advice and have found it good.

The trackers were quite discouraged, and declared that we had so alarmed the reindeer that they would not settle down to graze anywhere near. So we decided to give up chasing the reindeer, and turned our attention to wild boar. We gathered up our cook and our camp equipment and set out for another locality.

We roamed about for some days before we found a herd of boars. And as trained dogs are very good for this sport, the Prince decided to invite a hunter who had two good hounds to join us; so he gave three young noblemen directions how to reach the hunter's house, which was several miles away. They rode off, and finally returned with the man and his dogs.

The dogs quickly succeeded in rounding up the boars and turned them into a thick wood. We all scrambled after as fast as we could on horseback, crushing through briars and heavy underbrush.

Soon I heard a terrific yelling and yapping in front of me. The hunter riding near me thought that the hounds were in a fight with the boars. We pushed on toward the noise, and on arrival at the spot found that a pack of wolves had jumped into the fight and actually eaten one of the dogs.

The other dog and the boars were nowhere to be seen. We shouted to our companions and soon everyone rode in. We scoured the thicket and the surrounding country, but did not succeed in finding the other dog.

The old hunter was made very downhearted by this accident. The Prince's very generous gift of silver did not cheer him. He told us that the dog that had been killed had been his best friend and had really fed and clothed the entire family for the last two years by his skill in capturing valuable furs and meat.

In our delay over the dog we entirely lost the boar. We were all angry, and felt that the wolves needed a good lesson for their impudence, so we set out on their trail. After we had succeeded in killing one big male wolf we felt better, and returned to camp to enjoy a good dinner.

The following day we turned toward Urga. The Prince had concluded that serious sport was impossible for such a large and hilarious party, and decided to be content with a forest picnic. We camped by rivers and by mountain streams; we told stories at night, and made ourselves healthily tired during the day by chasing whatever animals we chanced to find. In this manner we took three days for the return trip and got back after what could not be called a very successful hunt, but we had all enjoyed ourselves immensely.

I have been on many other hunting trips with the Prince of Hanta when we secured much game — bears, wild asses, mountain goats, as well as wolves, deer, and boars. He was an expert long-distance shot, and wise in the secrets of forest and mountain.

In 1908 the Prince of Hanta asked me to go with him on a trip from Urga to Peking, then to Tientsin and on to Shanghai. The Prince had never been to sea before. He was much interested in our boat. We had a two-berth cabin together. I asked him to choose whether he would sleep in the upper or the lower berth. This matter occupied his mind for a long time.

He had never slept in a bed of any kind, as the Mongols always sleep on rugs thrown on the ground or on the floor of their yurtas or palaces. He pressed his hands on the berths, tried the springs, shook his head dubiously, and finally decided he would try to sleep in one of them; and when he had decided that, he gave his attention to the decision as to which it should be.

He said: "If I take the lower berth you will be above me, which is not quite right, as I am above you in rank." I agreed with him in this, but told him that it depended on which way we looked at it — whether the upper or the lower berth should by right go to the man of highest rank. Still, in case the steamer sank, the man in the upper berth would be nearer the surface of the sea.

He scratched his head over this for a little time, and then said: "Yes, if I were in the lower berth I might be drowned." So he took the upper berth, climbed into it, and there he stayed for the entire journey to Shanghai. The rough coastal trip he declared to be worse than any Mongolian blizzard.

When we got to Shanghai the steamer docked on the opposite side of the river from the city. We had to cross in a small sampan. He was very frightened by this and inquired how he would be able to save himself in case the sampan sank. I told him there was nothing to do but swim for the shore, and explained to him as best I could what swimming was. He said it would be impossible for him ever to learn to swim, and asked if there was some aid by which a man could keep himself afloat in the water until rescued.

I told him the only thing for that was a good lifebelt. He was much interested, and immediately we arrived on shore in Shanghai he insisted on going to a shop that sold lifebelts, where he ordered a hundred! These he shipped up to the plains of Mongolia, where they are probably in some yurta to-day.

When the Prince got back to Urga he unwrapped one of the lifebelts and showed it to the Living Buddha. The Buddha was most anxious to discover whether or not it really would work, so as the River Tola was in high flood they strapped it on to a lama priest and threw him in. He did not sink. The Prince of Hanta declared that the money spent for the lifebelts was really well invested.

Once the Prince stepped off the curb to cross

Nanking Road in Shanghai right in front of a street car which was coming at a good pace. I grabbed him and tried to pull him back. Then, when he would not come back, I attempted to hurry him across. He stopped dead and said: "Don't be a fool. I know how these cars are made. They have brakes and can be stopped at any place — so why hurry?"

In Shanghai the Prince of Hanta bought twenty thousand dollars' worth of stuff for the Dalai Lama, who was then in Peking. This was a most extraordinary business. He gave no order for any particular thing. He made all his purchases in three days, and spent the whole sum on foreign objects. Morning and afternoon of each day he asked me to conduct him to a foreign shop. Inside, he pointed the butt of his riding whip to everything that took his fancy and ordered it to be wrapped up and dispatched to Peking.

He bought, among other things, clocks, watches, looking-glasses, knives, canes, rugs, lamps, lanterns, a big astronomical telescope, a kitchen range, an electric curling iron, ladies' shoes with high heels, and a Christmas tree with decorations!

He was a riot in the shops. I could not curb his purchases or advise him in any single matter. He was like a child let loose in a bazaar. I did not think much of the things he got, but the Dalai Lama was very pleased, and so were all his friends whom he invited in to see what he had brought from the strange Chinese port city of Shanghai.

The Prince of Hanta had a son, the young Duke of Hanta, whom I met when I first went to Urga. He was my most intimate friend until his death a few years ago. He was an intelligent, clever companion. His death was brought about in the following way.

When the Dalai Lama was exiled from Tibet he sought refuge in North Mongolia. He stayed for a time at Urga, but as the revenue from pilgrims there did not amount to enough to satisfy both him and the Living Buddha, he had again to move. The Prince of Hanta invited him to rest in his state, two hundred miles to the northwest of Urga. While the Dalai Lama was there the young Duke of Hanta became his special favorite.

The Duke was of amiable disposition and very wealthy in his own right, so the Dalai Lama found him a valuable addition to his already numerous train. When the Dalai Lama moved to Wu-Tai-Shan in Shansi, he asked the Duke to accompany him; and although the Duke was reluctant to leave his homeland, he did not feel that he could refuse the recognized head of his religion. Later, the Dalai Lama moved from Shansi to Peking and took up his residence in the Yellow Temple outside the North Gate. He still kept the Duke in attendance.

I was often in Peking at that time, and I saw that the life in the capital of China was not the thing for this son of the wide spaces. I begged him to get permission from the Dalai Lama to go back home. He persisted in the statement that he was all right, and refused to go before the Dalai Lama should return to his own home in Tibet.

I went up to Mongolia and came back to Peking after several months. The Duke looked exceedingly ill. He coughed badly, was frail and thin. I begged him again to leave, but he refused. He came, however, to the station to see me off when I started north again. I took his arm and walked up and down the platform with him.

When the train pulled in I urged him to jump on and come back to Mongolia with me before it was too late. He refused, saying that his cough was a slight indisposition and that he would soon be all right. I never saw him again. He died in Peking a few weeks later.

This same thing has happened over and over again to strong and healthy Mongols I have known who have gone to Peking or to Tientsin for some reason or other. They have taken sick and died before they were able to get back home.

I have been exceedingly healthy all my life, but during the years that I was Mongolian representative and adviser on Mongolian affairs to the Government of China and was compelled to live for the most part of the year in Peking I suffered from continuous physical ailments. Sons of the high altitude and of the open life of the plains cannot live healthily in the crowded artificial cities.

Another Mongolian nobleman who was my friend for many years was Prince Lob-Tsen Yen-Tsen. He had a very comfortable residence five miles west of Urga. When he was a very small boy his parents sent him to a temple, where he was brought up as a lama. He passed through the various examinations that made him a priest of high degree. Then he left the temple, let his hair grow, became a "black man," and married a beautiful, well-educated Mongolian girl.

He held important positions in the Urga Government at various times during the last thirty-five years, but between these appointments he was often free. Then he could come and go at will. In his free times and mine we had many delightful holidays together. I think, as both of us were usually busy men, we enjoyed them more than do folk who can play all the time.

He was fond of hunting, and we two would often set off alone in midwinter for the mountains. There we would dig through the snow under the brow of a hill and make our camp.

Sometimes the snow was deep and we would have to dig down three or four feet. We always scooped it away to the ground, then built a fire of dry logs in the middle of the space; round the fire we laid heavy felt and furs. Here, no matter how many degrees below zero the thermometer dropped, or how hard the wind howled over the hilltops, we would be quite cosy. We would lie and talk of important matters which we could not discuss privately in Urga, and, when they were settled, tell fantastic stories until late hours.

On one of these occasions I had an accident which put me in a serious predicament. I woke up toward morning and smelled the odor of burned cloth — and discovered that my trousers were on fire. The most important part had already gone.

On these pleasure trips we carried no extra clothes

THE DUKE OF HANTA AND LOB-TSEN YEN-TSEN

and had with us no materials for mending; we never took pack animals with us, and the going was hard for the horses we rode, so we never took an extra thing. Lob-Tsen Yen-Tsen woke up and saw my predicament. He laughed heartily and wondered how I should be able to chase wolves on the morrow in weather so far below zero without any seat to my trousers. But when daylight came I found a piece of string in my coat pocket. With this I fastened a towel around my waist, then put on my trousers and was quite all right. My friend, in after days, was always very fond of telling his friends how I had burned my trousers and hunted wolves in a towel in midwinter.

Wolf hunting was the usual sport of these excursions. We rose early. After a light breakfast we saddled our horses, which had fed on the long grass from which they had scraped away the snow, and were off for whatever excitement we could find. Many a big grey wolf lost his pelt to us.

Prince Lob-Tsen Yen-Tsen was a very wealthy man. He had large herds of horses that he kept on the plain in his state to the south of Urga. We often went down there when we wanted to get away from Urga. We would amuse ourselves with horse races in which we took part with the herdsmen, or with wrestling matches between his men, and enjoyed many a fox hunt.

I was always made welcome in his home in Mai-Mai-Ch'ieng. I used to stay there for months at a time. I came and went as one of the family.

The saddest piece of news I had during the time

I was on the Chinese scientific expedition last winter with Sven Hedin was that Prince Lob-Tsen Yen-Tsen had died. His wife is still living. She is of the scholarly type, an intelligent, quiet thinker, and reads and writes the Mongolian language well. She always did her best to make my visit pleasant. I planned to go to see her when I returned from the expedition, but have not been able to do so yet.

The most outstanding personality among the Mongolian nobles that I have known was Prince Tsereng Dorch'i. He was for the last twenty years of his life the ruling spirit of North Mongolia. As Minister of Foreign Affairs he was a very shrewd diplomat, speaking and reading Chinese as easily as Mongolian. He was simple and hard-working. His character was so without blemish that he was asked to serve through all the political changes that have taken place in the Mongolian Government. He was Prime Minister under the old Manchu rule; he continued during the time of the Living Buddha's monarchy.

Then came the régime of the Chinese general, Little Hsu. Prince Tsereng Dorch'i remained Prime Minister. Next came Baron Ungern, the White Russian general, and his rule. Still Prince Tsereng Dorch'i, although he offered to resign, remained at his post. He served even under the Soviet directorate. He was Prime Minister until his death a year ago.

Prince Tsereng Dorch'i visited both Peking and Moscow. He was an intelligent conversationalist on many matters, and well read in the customs and the habits of other peoples and other countries.

When I first went to Mongolia he was a teacher
for the Russian consular students at Urga. He became my friend at that time, and he remained my
true friend always.

Although he had immeasurable power, — for he
decided almost every question of great importance
that came up during twenty years, — he lived and
dressed very simply. I used often to go to see him
in the yurta where he lived with his wife and son.
They did not have even a single servant. His wife
did the work of homemaking, just as any common
Mongolian woman would do. She used always to
brew fresh tea when she saw me coming, and gave
it to me with her own hands. He drew an almost
insignificant salary from the country. He had no
private wealth. He could have made a fortune for
himself, but it was beneath him to take for his work
any more than a bare subsistence.

At Christmas I generally sent him a box of candles,
for which his wife was extremely thankful. She used
always to tell me that it was exactly what she wanted
— ordinarily she had only basins of sheep tallow with
a horsehair wick as a light.

When his son married, the Prince did not even have
the necessary funds for his share of the wedding
expenses, although the wedding was a very simple
affair. He approached me and asked me whether I
would buy some of the presents he had received from
various foreign friends, as he absolutely needed the
money. This I did.

It always gave me a great deal of pleasure to sit
down and talk with Prince Tsereng Dorch'i. He was

one of the great men of the world. Other men —
wealthy nobles and high lamas — came to call on
him humbly, because they knew that although he
was not surrounded by material wealth he had a
spirit which enriched men who came near to him. He
used often to come to see me, always on a little pony
as any Mongol might have come.

He disliked show and waste of any kind. In his
management of government affairs he was as carefully economical as in his private life.

North Mongolia was indeed fortunate to have
such a man at the helm for many years.

Most of the young noble folk of Mongolia are not
interested in political or foreign affairs. They live a
serene life on the plains, identical with the life their
forefathers have lived for many centuries. But a few
of them have become interested in the outside world
and have gone abroad to study in foreign schools.
There are sons and daughters of my Mongolian
friends in Moscow, Berlin, Paris, and London. Most
of them stay only a short time, and are homesick
for the way of life on the plateau every hour of their
exile.

A young princess, the sister of the Prince of Palata
and grandniece of the Karasha Living Buddha, is an
example. When I passed through Peking last winter
on my way from Mongolia to Sweden I called on her
at the request of her relatives, to deliver messages
from them. She had been five years abroad, and
divided the time between Germany, France, England,
and China. She had learned to read and speak the

languages of these countries and to look very smart
in Parisian clothes.

Fair-complexioned, petite and vivacious, she greeted
me dressed in a white and cherry costume with
a chic little hat pulled down low on her brow.
I spoke in Mongolian. Her foreign fashionableness
slipped away like a cloak and she was just a little
child, homesick for her native air.

"I wanted to go abroad," she explained. "I have
gone and seen. There is no life in other parts of the
world like the wonderful life of my own people."

A few weeks later she capably got together a camel
caravan and started over the long route to her home
on the borders of Turkestan.

I have written this chapter in the Palace of the
Prince of Sunit. As I read it through I feel that I
have failed to put into words the calm courage and
the charming courtesy of the Mongolian nobles.
Familiarity here has dulled my sense for recording
the small things of which everyday life is made up.

I have known the Prince of Sunit since he was a
little boy. I knew his father who ruled before him.
And I knew also his uncle, who was a very influential
man in the capital of Mongolia, Urga, twenty-five
years ago, and regent here after his brother's death,
when the present Prince was too small to assume
authority.

Two weeks ago, as I sighted the obe on the highest
rise of hill above the residence of my host, I felt as
one always does when coming to the home of old,
well-known friends.

As we passed over the hill I saw the Prince and his brother, the head lama of the Sunit State Lamassery, worshiping the God of Earth at the obe, in the hope that prayers sent forth here would bring much-needed rain into the state, so that the horses, camels, cattle, sheep, and goats would have good grass on which to pasture this summer.

This obe is a mound of stones, with Tibetan prayers and saints' charms buried in a bucket deep in its heart. It was built by ancestors of the present ruler. Below the obe the curved and serrated roofs of the grey stone palace are outlined against the sky. A cluster of white felt yurtas on which are emblazoned the gold and blue dyed leather colors of the House of Sunit surround the Palace.

The Prince's mother came out to welcome me, accompanied by the little heir apparent, a lad of ten years. We exchanged formal greetings and she led me to a courtyard within the Palace where a suite of rooms had been made ready for my visit.

In Sunit, as in all other states of Mongolia, the people of the state serve in the Palace in rotation and as they are called, for a month at a time. So two men had been called in to serve me during my visit. They took my luggage, brought me fresh water to wash, and carried out the Dowager Mother's order that a hot meal should be cooked for me at once. Then while my meal was being prepared she sat down and we exchanged information concerning her children and their children and my six sons and daughters and grandchildren.

The men brought my meal. Here in Sunit, as in

most monarchs' residences, servants put on "the hat of food ceremony" when they serve food. This is a hat with a peaked crown, with a long red silk fringe hanging down all round. Each basin of food is presented on the flat palms of two hands, the serving man bending one knee and saying, "Please take the food, and peace be with you as you eat it."

When the meal is finished, one thanks the servant for it and says, "Please take up the food." In a ruler's residence this would be impossible, as the supply is so lavish. The food that is left belongs by right to one's serving men, and is ample for them to feast on during all the time of their service.

In Mongolia, except at a time of feast, the entire family or all the people in residence at an encampment do not eat together in one big crowd. Here in Sunit my meals are usually served to me alone, although occasionally the Prince, or his mother, or his son, or some visiting noble, dines with me.

Mongolian tea — that is, tea made with milk, butter, and salt — is served the first thing in the morning; and the Dowager Mother, who knows my appetite for milk, either mare's or cow's, always sends me a generous pail of milk every morning in addition to my tea. The first real meal of the day is just before noon; the second is just before sunset.

The first day I arrived here I had a big meal, by order of the Dowager Mother, in mid-afternoon. I was hungry from a long ride and ate well, so that when evening came I did not want food again, except a little milk and cheese. I told my serving men not to put the food on my table.

They answered: "You are our monarch's honored guest; your food is cooked in his private kitchen; we must put it down, or we shall be reprimanded by the Prince because we did not serve you a hot meal at sunset. When we put it down you can order us to take it up again." I had to remove my writing papers from the table, let them put the food bowls on it, and then order them to take it up again, with the usual ceremony.

The father of the present ruler of Sunit had three wives. The first died without offspring. Then he married a princess from a neighboring state, a very beautiful girl in her early twenties — and a very beautiful woman now, although fifty-eight years of age. She has a smooth, fair skin, unwrinkled by time, a laughing, happy nature, and very modern ideas.

For instance, she sent to Germany for tiles, pipes, and white porcelain fittings and had Chinese workmen come from Peking and build her a modern bathroom in one corner of her apartments in the palace. This is the only bathroom of which I have ever heard in a Mongolian home.

The Mongols have a superstition that anyone who bathes all over at one time will turn into a fish. This dates back to a law from Genghis Khan's time which forbade the use of water for washing, since it must be conserved for men and herds to drink. The enforcement of this law was ensured by building up superstitious religious myths around it. There was great consternation not only among the Princess's serving women and her immediate family but in neighboring states because she brought a bathtub into her apartments. Friends came from far and near and begged her not to make use of it. She bravely had a bath the day the room was finished, and has bathed every day during the five years since then.

She laughingly explained to me to-day: "I am not a fish yet. The Prince has been so impressed that he also has bathed himself twice all over. And he has not turned into a fish either. But his mother has given him an order not to do it again, lest he have to be a fish in the next world as a punishment for swimming about in a tub of water when water is really needed to make grass grow."

I had scarcely finished my first meal on arrival at the Palace when this princess, second wife to the late ruler, came in to visit me. As always, she was dressed in lovely silk, with pearls and golden ornaments on her wrists and in her hair. She is possessed of the graceful ease which comes natural to a woman who has been at home in the palaces of Mongols and Manchus, on the plateau and in China, all her life.

This second wife, like the first, bore the ruler of Sunit no offspring. The people of the state were anxious concerning the future: a descendant of Genghis Khan, in direct male descent, had always sat on their throne. Finally the late ruler took as wife the daughter of a wealthy commoner whose family were noted for the fertility of their women. She bore two sons, one of them the present monarch of Sunit.

Between this buxom woman and the beautiful Princess there is always a dignified reserve. The

Prince's mother lives in her yurta beyond the palace gates and looks after the material details of the state as carefully as though she had need of every lamb. The Princess presides at all social functions. It was she who went to the Manchu court to represent the state socially at Peking. She speaks and reads Mandarin fluently, and has a quick wit.

As I sat visiting with her on the afternoon of my arrival a murmur ran from lip to lip through the Palace: "The ruler has come home, and is changing his garments ready to welcome the visitor."

The Prince of Sunit is a tall, thin young man of thirty years — a quiet, serious, kindly ruler who has a firm grip on affairs when firmness is needed. The affairs of his state are always in perfect order. There is almost no poverty here. One can travel day after day through Sunit without meeting a single person who does not possess a good felt tent, at least one cow to give milk, some sheep, goats, and a horse or two.

The Prince of Sunit's standing army is well drilled and in good order. Every man in Sunit comes in to the Palace once every year for instruction and observation. The Prince encourages his men to keep fit by wrestling, and every evening the Sunit men wrestle on the greensward at the Palace. Even the lamas in this state could be called upon for military service if they were needed to defend it.

Russia and China are both bidding for favor in Inner Mongolia; the princes of Inner Mongolia know that their independent position will keep these Powers vying with each other in petitions for favor just so long as they maintain sufficient strength to thwart outside Powers.

When the Prince came he talked with me, first about intimate personal matters, covering the usual exchange of information about each other since we had last met. Then he told me that his great concern was what attitude to take in regard to the invitation of the Nationalist Government of China for peaceful and amiable coöperation with them. The Prince of Sunit feels keenly the responsibility that rests upon him in politics, since he has been asked by the rulers of ten independent Mongol states to act as their leader in all conferences with foreign countries.

While we talked of politics, the little ten-year-old heir apparent leaned against my knee, occasionally putting in a question which shows that even now he has the same keen mind as his father and his grandfather. The father's patience in answering his questions was in keeping with the manner in which Mongol rulers bring up their heirs, training them to be ready to assume responsibility, if necessary, at a very early age. They never answer "Wait until you are older" to any question, but as soon as the child has intelligence to ask a question they assume that he has the mind to understand the answer.

After an hour of serious talk, the Prince said: "Let us now put aside these things until another day; you have had a hard, long journey. We will go and watch the wrestlers." After that he and I joined the commoner who is now acting here as Chief at the Yamen and went to watch the wrestling which is an every-evening performance at Sunit Palace.

The Prince of Sunit's wrestlers are always dressed in soft green dyed-leather sleeveless jackets with short gold silk breeches and high leather boots. These garments are decorated with flat gold buttons; they are kept neatly folded away in a storeroom in the Palace when not in use.

As we came back from the wrestling we passed oxen dragging round-bellied water carts up from the well. The supply of water is drawn from the well twice daily, morning and evening. In addition to the carts used for this the Prince of Sunit has several hundred oxcarts put in neat rows in one of the Palace courtyards ready for use when he needs to send out into the state for supplies.

Pitched round the Palace there are two or three dozen white felt yurtas. The Prince's mother dwells in the largest of these, which is ornamented with designs of gold and blue dyed leather. Here she is bringing up the little heir apparent. Other tents house various relatives and workmen and women who have come in from the country to serve their allotted month in the ruler's residence. Some of these women are always busy mending the blue traveling tents that herdsmen use. They sit on the grass, laughing and talking, as they work. Other women take care of the milk and the butter.

The ropes for tying up the cows when they are milked are stretched not far from the yurta of the Prince's mother. She is always up at sunrise when the cows are first milked, and on hand for the second milking at sunset.

She superintends the care of the milk, the making

of butter and cheese, and the storing away of supplies for winter. She sees to it that the argol stacks are sufficient to provide all necessary fires, and superintends the making of felt and the curing of skins and furs.

She has her own herds, and gives minute directions to her herdsmen concerning their care. She seems to know every animal in the state of Sunit. If one mentions a horse with a white sock observed in a herd two days' journey from the Palace, she nods her head and tells some detail about that particular animal. Horses are always tied at the hitching place in front of Sunit Palace, saddled and bridled ready for the immediate use of anyone who happens to need one for an errand.

There has been little rain so far this season, and grass is scarce although it is June, a time when it is usually thick. All the animals, except those which are needed for daily use here, have been driven to other parts of the state where there has been more rainfall. Several of my days here have been spent visiting the herds. When we ride through the country the people of the state whom we pass dismount and kneel while we ride by, but aside from this formal courtesy there is a genial democratic comradeship between the rulers of Sunit and the people.

Whether out in the country or at the Prince's residence, the last hour of the day before sunset is a relaxed hour in which we often have music on the flute, singing, or a minstrel to chant some old historic story.

The Prince is preparing to go in state with a

magnificent mounted guard to meet the Panchan Lama, who is coming into Sunit to visit. As he will be thus occupied, he has selected his cousin to confer with the Nationalist Government and is making arrangements for him to go down to Nanking.

This cousin, a Mongolian duke, is a fine scholar in Tibetan, Chinese, and Mongolian. He passed a Chinese literary examination with honors in 1895, and held a position at the court of the Chinese Empress Dowager, with the privilege of wearing the peacock feather and the sapphire button.

But before the Prince of Sunit or his cousin leaves, the State Fair is to be held. At this fair there will be the usual wrestling matches, horse races, and display of gorgeous raiment. In addition to the people of Sunit, the rulers of neighboring states have sent dispatch riders in to say that they too will come to the fair. It will give them an opportunity both for sport and for the discussion of important matters.

The Mongol will do no work that is a variation from the accepted needs of Mongolian life. This palace with its many courtyards is an imported idea, and thus no Mongol can be relieved from his annual month of service when it must be made ready for the fair. Workmen have been brought in from China, and are regilding the brilliant pillars, touching up the gate lions with fresh ferociousness, and cleaning the mosaics under the eaves of the curved roofs.

Mongol workers are occupied putting up festival tents, selecting fat sheep for the feasts, brewing wine from mare's milk, choosing horses and jockeys for the races, and making ready fine raiment for themselves and their ruler and his family.

Everyone is preparing to enjoy the annual fair, except the young wife of the monarch of Sunit, who is secluded in a quiet place. The people of Sunit pray that in six more months she may be delivered of a son who will make more certain the lineal descent of the throne.

Minstrels chant softly of the coming of another Temujin. The expectant mother may not go abroad or receive visitors, but must wait alone, holding her mind in pure contemplation of those thoughts which it is believed will make the child intelligent and brave.

II
THE PEOPLE

The Mongol people are a happy, merry people in time of peace; cool and collected in time of trouble. They live simple, outdoor lives, and feed on plain, wholesome food. Although they are a very old race and were once the conquerors of half the world, they have never adopted or evolved a complex system of life. I have lived among them in commoner's yurta and monarch's palace for thirty-five years. I am filled with admiration of their honorable simplicity.

Genghis Khan, accompanied by his brothers, by his sons, and by thousands of followers, went into Europe. They had opportunity to observe how luxuriously the peoples they conquered lived. But during the years of conquest the Mongols dwelt in their own tents or kept themselves hard by the same activities as when on the Mongolian plateau. They never moved into the cities they captured. While they marveled at the multitudes of comforts Europeans possessed, still they reasoned, "Since we have beaten these peoples so easily, they must be weakened by their civilization." This is the explanation that Mongolian folklore gives.

When the Mongols returned to their homeland they entered contentedly the yurtas where their women and children had carried on during their absence: they made no attempt to change the system of life from what it had always been. Genghis Khan's grandson, Kublai Khan, became Emperor of China, but he did not copy the complex civilization of the land he ruled.

So through the centuries, if one believes the stories Mongols tell, life has remained the same on the Mongolian plateau; unchanged by contact with Russia which presses on the north, by China on the south, or by any information concerning life outside that leaks in. The Mongol is quick to listen concerning the ways of other countries. But he does not adopt them.

The Mongolian people are never overworked, because their needs are few. They never rush or hurry over anything, but take the full joy out of every hour as it passes. They never have any exciting telegrams, express letters, or newspapers. They have no trains to catch, no office hours to keep. They are not weakened by overheated rooms, luxurious furniture, soft beds, or big dinners at which the stomach has to digest innumerable kinds of rich food. They have no narrow streets and no troublesome traffic regulations. They never suffer nervous breakdown.

When I was younger I believed implicitly in the civilization of the West as superior to anything else in the world. I have spent hours talking to Mongolian princes and commoners, attempting to persuade them to build railways, start postal services, and found newspapers.

Invariably I have met with the same retort: "All these things may be good in other countries; but

we do not need them here. We are happy and content as we are. A postal service would bring in
letters from outside — trouble us with all sorts of
things. I do not need letters. None of my people
need letters. If anyone wants to communicate with
me or I with him, life is not too short for either of
us to get on a horse and go to the other. Letters
would mean that we should bother each other with
all sorts of trivial matters. It is better so. A man does
not travel a month on horseback for a trivial matter,
but he does if he has a real need to see a friend."

I remember another time, when I went to stay
with a very intelligent Mongol prince in Inner
Mongolia. It was several years after the end of the
World War. He had not yet heard that the war had
started. When I told him that if he had had a news-
paper printed in his state then he would have known
what was going on in the world, he retorted: "Why
should I know any sooner than you have told me?"

The Mongol people are tall, lithe, and strong.
They have a dashing, slightly devil-may-care grace,
and a quick humor which twinkles in their eyes.
Their hair and eyes are dark. Their complexion
would be fair, but continuous exposure to wind and
sun tans their faces and hands to a deep bronze.

The garb of men, women, and children, whether
commoner or noble, is practically the same. They
wear trousers and shirt under a long outer garment
slit on the sides so as not to hamper them when in
the saddle. Men and unmarried girls have the long
garment bound with a wide girdle. This girdle is a

length of silk wound several times about the waist. Married women wear their outer garment hanging free. Everyone wears high riding boots of stout leather, turned up at the toe tip to suit the Mongolian stirrup. The tops are high and have a pocket in them for the man's pipe or for any article the woman may desire to carry there.

The garments are fashioned of cotton, of silk, or of fur in winter. The robes of priests are of crimson or yellow, and those of the lay folk are of every other color. The Mongols have a harmonious color sense, and blend bright hues together wonderfully. They never use shades of color, but always pure primary colors.

Fashions do not change in Mongolia, but continue the same through the centuries, so that festival dresses are often handed down from generation to generation. With the passage of years they seem to take on more lovely tones than they had when they were new.

Lamas have their heads shaven and wear gay-colored caps of various designs, but they usually have two long ribbon streamers which float behind. Laymen wear their hair in a long black plait reaching, often, below the waist. In winter they wear close-fitting caps of bright color, perhaps with a squirrel's tail curled rakishly over one ear; in summer, a wide-brimmed hat, faced with some pretty color and tied under the chin with ribbons to keep it from blowing off when galloping across the plain on horseback.

Young girls part their hair in the middle and plait it down their backs. Married women keep their hair long. They dress it in neat coils on the head in Inner Mongolia, in smooth wide wings in Outer Mongolia. Every married woman has an elaborate headdress. This is the dowry which she receives from the father when she marries, and is valuable in proportion to his wealth.

Noblewomen have headdresses of gold set with rubies, emeralds, and pearls, often with a long curtain of jewels, which hangs to the waist behind, set in a network of gold. Commoners' headdresses are of silver, with the stones according to the wealth of the woman's family. Every feminine headdress has deep old-rose coral set in it. Coral is the national ornament of Mongolia. Some women use no ornamentation except lovely pieces of coral that have been handed down from the generations, set in silver. Every woman also has a snuff bottle made of gold or silver, and ornamented with coral and jewels.

Every Mongol man, whether lama or layman, wears a long knife, thrust through his girdle on his right side. These knives are carried in a sheath which also contains a socket in which chopsticks are carried. Attached to each sheath is a chain with a heavy ornament. The chain is twisted through the girdle and the end ornament keeps it from slipping out. Knife sheath and chain are of gold or silver studded with precious stones, according to the wealth and fancy of the owner. On the left side every man wears a flint purse with a chain and end ornament to match those on the knife.

Each man also has a snuff bottle, larger in size than the woman's, which he carries in his girdle.

Each person in Mongolia has his or her own food bowl. These are of birch-root wood, often gold- or silver-lined and with gold or silver ornamentation on the outside. No person in Mongolia goes abroad without taking his food bowl with him. It is carried in the front of his or her garment.

The Mongolian people dwell in a cone-shaped structure which foreigners call a "yurta" and the Mongols a "gerr." The inside framework is a criss-cross lattice of wood, generally willow, bound together with short rawhide thongs. These press up into a small bundle for transport. When a yurta is set up, men stretch out four to eight of these sections, according to the size desired, so as to form a circular wall about four feet high. An opening is left on the south side in which is placed a carved door frame.

Next, two workers stand in the centre of the circle and hold a wheel on poles high above their heads. Other poles are stuck slantingly into slots in the wheel with their lower ends fitted into leather loops at the top of the lattice. This makes a skeleton cone. Over this skeleton cone, with care to leave the wheel uncovered, the workers put three or four layers of wool felt, which are shaped to fit the cone, and fasten them with horsehair rope.

Then the two-panel door is hung in the door frame by fitting the two whittled points at the outer side of each panel into socket holes in the frame. Lastly, a neat square of felt is arranged over the wheel with a rope attached to it so that the felt can be thrown back or pulled over by a person standing on the ground. This felt is never entirely closed. The opening serves as an outlet for smoke from the fire which is placed directly under it.

Set on the greensward, these neat cone-shaped dwellings are a picturesque sight.

Yurtas all over Mongolia are built in exactly the same way. This is the pattern handed down through the centuries. The structure is so much a matter of routine to every Mongol from childhood that he can take one down in half an hour or set it up again in the same time.

It is the custom in the autumn to renew half of the yurta felt. In the last mild days of summer the felt is taken off the yurtas, shaken, and the bad pieces discarded. Then it is put on again with what was the back top layer now the front top layer, with new felt at the back.

A yurta is a comfortable abode in which to live. It is cool in summer, as the felt keeps out the burning Mongolian sun, and yet is so put on that it can be rolled up as high as one wishes around the bottom, to let in fresh air. In winter it is snug and warm, as neither wind nor rain penetrates through it. It is a curious thing, but when in a felt yurta, unless the door is open, one is not disturbed by any noises outside. Even the howling of the wind in the fiercest blizzard is not heard.

A Mongolian housewife does not waste time seeking the best way to arrange the interior of any of the family yurtas, because custom decrees exactly where every article of furniture shall be put. The

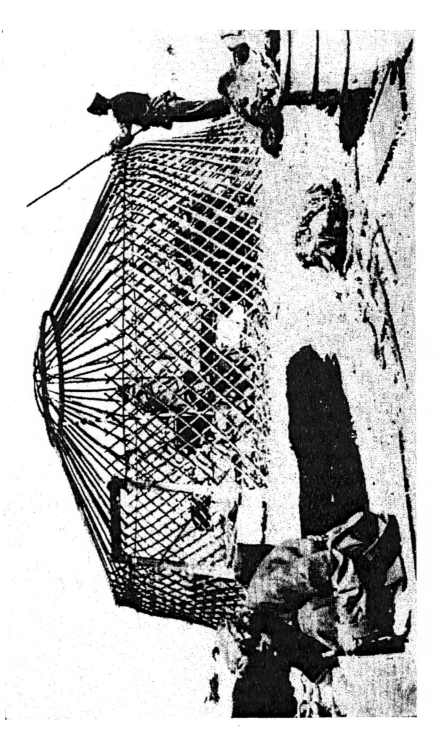

THE WOODEN FRAMEWORK OF A YURTA

less well-off families have to make a single yurta serve as kitchen, living room, and bedroom.

In such a yurta all the household utensils are in upright cupboards on the left side of the entrance door. Opposite the door, on the northwest side of the yurta the shrine is placed, with its small gods, images of Buddha and his disciples, butter lamps, incense burners, and small cups for sacrificial wine. On the north side of the yurta stands a low framework called a bedstead, although it is not slept on, but used to hold the family bedclothes when they are not in use.

Next to this are placed the floor cushions, ready to be used when one wants to sit down. These are generous-sized squares backed with felt two or three inches thick and faced with red cloth. They are manufactured in Tibet, and are of lovely color and design. Beyond the heap of cushions are chests to hold garments, furs, and different things. The Mongolian home is small, and each article in it has a place. The people are very careful to keep their things neat and tidy. This habit makes it easy for them to move quickly.

The yurta floor is covered with thick felt quilted in a stitch pattern. In the very centre of the tent the ground is left bare; the quilted felt padding is cut off neatly to make a centre bare circle, and is usually worked around in a kind of buttonhole design with black horsehair, which makes an attractive finish. The centre floor is packed down hard. In this square stands the Mongolian stove — four uprights of iron held together by three rings. It is always big and strong enough to hold a huge iron pot.

In this iron brazier the fire of argol is lit. Argol burns with very little smoke, so that little finds its way out through the hole in the top of the yurta. Mongolian women are skillful in raising the exact piece of felt in the wall covering which will make a draught that will carry the smoke up in a straight line.

The low cupboards, altar, and chests made of hand-carved wood decorated with bright painted pictures of flowers and animals, the flickering flames of the butter lamps on the polished silver altarpieces, the gay carpet cushions laid on the quilted felt floor, and the red glow of the argol fire with its warm light throwing into relief the smooth birch framework of the tent in black lines against the white felt, make an inviting picture when one gets down from a hard day in the saddle.

The Mongols do not pitch their tents together in clusters like village groups. Each family stands its tents alone, so the number placed together depends upon the wealth of the particular family. It varies from one to twenty. Wealthy people have a kitchen tent in which all the cooking is done, a guest tent for the entertainment of visitors, a tent in which to house their gods and hold services on the special festival days of the year, with as many more yurtas as they need for their personal comfort. The Mongols do not like crowding and prefer a yurta each if they are single, or one to each man and wife, with perhaps their small children in with them, if married. The poor have to lie down, guests and family together, in a single tent. Each individual tent is furnished as described, as each person has his own altar and likes a pot on the fire in case he wants a meal in private.

In front of each family encampment, whether it comprises one tent or twenty, there are always two pillars thrust into the ground with a thong of rawhide stretched between them. This is the hitching place for horses. The Mongols never walk if they can ride. Religious pilgrims walk thousands of miles, but except to win favor from Heaven the Mongol will not move even a few steps on foot if he can possibly avoid it.

The hitching place is provided not only for guests but for saddled and bridled horses that stand always ready for use. Man, woman, or child would not think of walking fifty yards to the well to fetch water, but will jump on a horse and trot down to it.

When my wife used to spend the summers with me in Tabo-ol she was often distressed by the work — or lack of work — which characterized the Mongol we employed as cook. I used to tell her that I was certain that the Mongol would be as good a cook as she could get anywhere in the world if she would just devise a kitchen in which he could do his work on horseback.

When a family have selected the pitch for their encampment, the first thing that is done is to put up a high pole and fasten on it silk ribbons that have been inscribed with Tibetan prayers. These are called "galloping wind horses." The people believe that the wind, fluttering the prayers banners, pleases the gods just the same as though a member of the family read the prayers aloud.

After the tents are pitched, a prayer wheel is attached to each one. The wind twirling the prayer wheel can serve in the place of a member of the family. This is supposed to assure the household of the favor of the local gods.

In addition to the horses which one finds in front of every Mongolian encampment, there are dogs — huge shaggy beasts with a ruff on their necks which gives them the appearance of a lion. These beasts are very fierce. It is their duty to guard the dwelling of their masters day and night.

The Mongols feed their dogs well and take excellent care of them. They are sturdy and brave, and do not fear to tackle wolves alone. In a land where wolves press as closely as they do here, it is absolutely necessary to have these kinds of dogs. But custom decrees that, when a visitor approaches, the inhabitants of an encampment must go out of a yurta and call off the dogs. They are quite harmless as soon as they see that the master or mistress welcomes the visitor. They will not make any show of friendliness, but remain neutral until the visit is over and the stranger is again mounted on his horse. Then they are fierce as upon his first arrival.

The Mongolian people are nomads. They move from place to place with their herds according to the abundance of grass and water. The continuous shift of the encampments leaves no part of the land scarred by human residence; clean grass grows quickly over every vacated camp site. The people in the south, as a rule, move only twice a year — into the open grazing country in the spring, and into a sheltered place under the brow of a hill in the winter. The people in the north move more often. They are less dependent on wells. In summer they graze the grass up and down the river. In winter when there is snow they move out into the plain or into the forest, just as pasture draws them. Mongolian herds are adept at pawing away snow, if it is not too deep, and getting at the hay which lies under the snow all winter.

All land in Mongolia is common or state land. No individual has a deed or right to any particular piece of it. It belongs equally to all the people of the state. The herds of nobles and commoners roam over it, grazing where they can and will, except that preference for place is governed by the common law that the first family to put up its tents by a well has the first right to stay there. Should the water run low the last comer has to be the first to move.

The water hole — that is, well or river bank where herds go down to drink — gives its name to the locality. When traveling through the country, if I want to find one of my friends and ask where he is, I am always answered by the name of the watering place and go there to find him. All roads in Mongolia lead in to the watering place. If lost, one has but to follow the first path until it is intersected by a second one, then to note which way the arrow of union points. The point shows the way to the well. At every well one may be fairly certain to find an encampment and a shelter for the night.

In South and Inner Mongolia, there are numerous

wells all over the country. One has only to dig a little way in the ground — from ten to twenty feet — to find water. Mostly the water is good and can be drunk directly from the well without hesitation. In a few places it is brackish or mixed with soda, so that it is nasty to the taste and impossible to use either for cooking food or for making tea. Heavy rains often spoil wells for a short time, as they wash in dust and make the water undrinkable.

At every well of good water one finds a long pole with a goatskin pail fastened to the end of it ready to be dipped down into the well and brought up filled with a sparkling icy drink. I always drink the water of Mongolia, just as my Mongolian friends drink it, fresh from the well, and have never suffered any ill effects from it. Every well has a long watering trough ready for use in watering animals.

The Mongols never place their yurtas above a well so that waste from them could drain down into it. It is the established custom for every family to camp a little way from the watering place.

In North Mongolia, large and small rivers as well as fresh running springs are abundant, so that very few wells have to be dug.

The Mongols do not till the soil, neither do they keep chickens or pigs. They are dependent upon their herds for the necessities of life. Consequently their principal work is the care of their horses, camels, cattle, goats, and sheep. All are running herds. Even sheep are tended by a man on horseback.

Men generally do the herding, except on those occasions when there is no man available because of

THE MONGOLIANS DO NOT PITCH THEIR TENTS IN VILLAGE GROUPS
EACH FAMILY STANDS ITS TENTS ALONE

war or illness. Aside from moving or repairs, the men do very little about the yurta. The herdsman camping with the animals out on the plains, in the blue cloth herd tent, does all his own simple housekeeping.

Boys are trained very young in the care of animals. There is usually a man and a boy in charge of every horse herd. Their duty is to see that the herd has good grass and water, and to watch the mares in the season of the arrival of the young colts. They have to be continuously on guard against wolves. Watching over the herd at night is not light work.

The herdsmen also break and train to the saddle all young animals. They generally select one or two of the speediest colts and train them in as lasso horses. For this only the most intelligent are selected, as the Mongol horseman demands that his mount work with him. The Mongolian lasso is a slender birch or willow pole about fifteen feet long, with a rope of rawhide at the end. The herdsman is too busy handling this implement to guide his horse.

He rides without the use of his reins, and it is marvelous how quickly a lasso horse discovers which horse it is his rider desires to catch. A lasso horse is trained so that immediately he knows which horse his master is after he gives chase in and out among hundreds of other horses until the man has the lasso over the horse's head. Then the lasso horse slackens his speed and braces himself until the other horse is forced to a stop.

A skillful lasso man does not throw the rawhide

loop of his lasso around the neck of the horse he wishes to catch, but across under the throat and up between the ears, which pulls the horse still very quickly.

I have a herdsman who throws his rawhide thong so that with two or three deft twists he makes a perfect halter around the horse's head.

Men out with the herds, day after day, months on end, grow exceedingly fond of their animals. It is difficult work in winter, in a strong blizzard, to keep the herd together. Often the men suffer extreme hardship, but I have yet to meet a Mongol who complained about weather.

One of my own herdsmen got lost in a blizzard and could not be found for three days. When we did find him, he told the following story: "The blizzard came up after dark — I was in the saddle the whole night. The herd held together, moving slowly with the wind. Toward noon the first day I came upon some yurtas. Here the people helped me from the saddle, thawed out my mount and me, and gave us food.

"During this delay the herd wandered a considerable distance away. When I caught them my mount was quite tired out, so I caught a young horse and let mine go free. That night I got the herd in the lee of a mountain. The second day and the third day have been about the same."

The man made no complaint about his hardship, but he was pleased when I made him a present of a good riding horse as his own.

Another time, when I was staying in the encampment of Mongol friends, a herdsman came walking in toward the yurtas. It had been a stormy night. My thermometer was so far below zero that it had ceased to work. This man told us that in order to assure himself of a good strong mount he had caught and saddled one of his big stallions the night before. But the herd had been stampeded by wolves. In the rush he had been thrown from the saddle, and lost the stallion. He asked our aid in helping him to find the stampeded horse herd.

My host had three horses lassoed from his own herds and brought in. We saddled and bridled them and rode out with the distressed man. After a search of nearly a day we found the herd all safe under the brow of a hill, except the stallion, who was nowhere in sight. The snow was deep and cut up by the hoofs of the five hundred horses in the herd. But finally we found a single track leading away from the others. Interlaced with the marks of the horse's hoofs were the tracks of a wolf. Ten miles away we found the stallion, and near him the trampled remains of a big grey male wolf. The horse was lathered with foam and still wet with sweat, although many hours had elapsed since the stampede.

It sometimes happens that herds of thousands of horses are lost in the blizzards, their herdsmen with them. No trace of either is found until the spring, when the deep snow melts away and their bodies tell the story of what has happened.

But despite the fierceness of the Mongolian winter I do not think it takes as heavy a toll of life as office work does in the big cities. A large percentage of the Mongolians live to a hale and hearty old age. Outdoor life is the healthiest life, and hard weather endured from birth produces a strong race.

The guarding of sheep is one of the easier tasks of Mongolian life. It is given usually to the old or to the very young. The sheep are folded in the home encampment every night. They are driven into an enclosure or guarded between the yurtas by men and dogs. In the lambing season the flock is kept very near to the encampment even during the day, because of the danger from wolves. At night the little lambs are sheltered in one or more of the yurtas emptied of all furniture for that purpose. Many a night I have been turned out of a big guest tent and asked to sleep with my host so that his baby sheep would have a good place to rest.

The Mongolian shepherd, mounted on a patient and gentle horse, drives his flock into the face of the wind in the morning and does not permit them to graze until they have reached a good distance from home. Then he turns them so that the wind is at their backs and helps them on their way home. At the end of the day, when they are tired, they do not have a long hard journey against the wind.

Cattle are not so numerous in Mongolia as one might suppose they would be in a rolling open country. But every family does keep a certain number of milk cows and some steers for winter meat, as well as oxen to use as pack animals and to draw carts. These are herded on the plains in the same way as the horses. Camels are bred and used to ride and to carry packs.

In addition to the care of the herds, there is the work of making tent felt from wool, curing skins for use as coats and rugs, tanning leather, and preparing rawhide. Men and women work together in the making of felt. After the wool has been sheared from the sheep it is worked thoroughly over with a bowstring until it is light and fluffy.

An old piece of felt of the same size and shape as is again desired is laid down on the clean grass. Wool is put on it, piled up to the thickness of several inches, and sprinkled all over with whey left from the cheese making. A long smooth pole is then laid across one end of the felt and around this the wool and the felt are rolled.

The roll is wrapped tightly with strings made from horsehair. When it is firm a long rope is fastened to each end of the poles in such a way that the pole can revolve without twisting up the rope. Then two men, riding on horseback, each take one of the ropes. They gallop side by side across the plain, turning this way and that, with the pole spinning behind them.

The rolling action presses the wool into felt. After about an hour the men gallop back to the encampment. The roll is untied and women work it all over with their hands, rubbing it smooth. Then they wet it again with cheese water, tie it up as before, and the men gallop another hour. This is done three or four times, until the felt is of good hard quality and sufficiently well knit to resist wind and rain. When it is dried it is ready for use.

In good weather, when the herds pasture peacefully, the herdsmen occupy themselves by making horsehair ropes. The Mongolian horses' manes grow so long that they straggle over their eyes, and their tails drag on the ground if not cut off. The herdsmen shear this long hair and use it for the making of ropes. It is twisted firm and tight, and it is as good a rope as one can find anywhere in the world — superior to hemp rope, in a country of heavy wet snow such as we have in Mongolia.

The tanning of skins as the Mongolian does it is a very simple matter. Whey from the cheese making is mixed with pure milk and soda, which one finds in abundance in Mongolia. The skin is pegged out on the ground and a little of this mixture is poured over it every morning for six or seven days. Then it is dried in the sun until quite stiff and hard. Next, the Mongols bury it in the earth, where it is left for a week or two. When taken out it is worked with a wooden comb until it becomes soft and pliable.

Now the tanner takes the big knife which he carries in a sheath at his right side and scrapes the skin until it is smooth. After this a small fire is built in a hole in the ground and the skin is arranged over it like a tent. When well smoked it is rubbed with soft sour cheese and scraped again with a knife. Then it is worked with the hands until soft and pliable and ready for use.

Wolf, fox, marten, and other furs used for coats are tanned in exactly the same way as leather prepared for saddles and boots.

Rawhide for halters, bridles, hobbles, straps, lasso

thongs, and for fastening yurtas together is made from oxhide. The hair is scraped off the skin, it is soaked in whey for a week, and then dried. When dry the strings are cut to the desired width. Then mutton fat is rubbed on it and it is worked to make it soft.

Every Mongol man needs to know a little about carpentry, but not much — just enough to make the framework for a yurta, or to hollow out a log for a watering trough. Tables, cupboards, altars, are handed down from generation to generation, so that if it happens that a man is born with skill in the use of his hands he usually provides his clan with enough of these things to last until another such craftsman comes along.

The Mongolian saddles are commonly made of birch, which must be grown curved so as to make a strong frame. This means the tree has to be bent a good many years before the saddle is made. After the wooden frame has been cut, according to the pattern which the plainsmen have used since the days of Genghis Khan, it is padded with cloth or leather and studded with silver and gold.

Silverwork is almost the only craft in Mongolia. There is a silversmith attached to every Mongolian nobleman's household; and plenty of craftsmen go from their own family encampments to make silver articles, when desired, in the encampments of neighbors and friends.

Silver and gold are both mined in Mongolia, but not in very large quantity as yet, although immeasurable wealth in these minerals lies beneath the rolling green plains. It has been the custom of centuries to take out only what happens to be needed at the time.

Every Mongolian woman has a heavy headdress. If she is a noblewoman, it is of gold; if a commoner, of silver. This is made in preparation for her wedding day by the craftsman who comes to her father's encampment for the purpose and makes it into just as beautiful a pattern as he can devise with the corals or the jewels that the family provide to set in it. Mongolian girls and women also wear silver bracelets, finger rings, and earrings, and they carry snuffboxes of solid silver.

Every man has a silver-handled knife, silver-handled chopsticks, both fitting into a heavy silver case, a silver flint case, knobs for his keys, saddle, bridle, and backstrap ornaments of silver. Many people have food basins gold- or silver-lined. Silversmiths take 40 per cent of the silver for their work. They do not have any designs except those which they carry in their heads.

The craftsman goes to the encampment where he is desired to work. Each member of the family who has a lump of silver and wants an article made talks with him about the design he or she would like. One wants antelopes in a grove of birches in relief on the bottom of his food bowl. Another desires the eight emblems of sacrifice in a circle round the wood. Another would like coral and jade set in the pattern of a flower on the two sides of his snuff bottle. A young girl wants a dragon twisted into a bracelet. A man would like the twelve animals of the zodiac on his knife sheath, so that he can keep track more easily of the name of the year.

When the silversmith knows what is wanted, he gets out his crucible for melting the metal and the tools for shaping it. The lump of pure gold or pure silver is handed over to him and he goes to work. The Mongol silversmith does beautiful, solid work, equal to any metal work that I have seen in any other place in the world.

Many Mongolian women are very good-looking, as fair as many of the races of Europe, with rosy complexions and masses of dark hair. The Mongolian woman does not age so quickly as the women of other Oriental races; she leads a free, open-air life.

The little Mongolian girl learns to ride astride as early as her young brother. Old Mongolian women ride just as well as old Mongolian men. The women of Mongolia have always been socially as free as the men. Housekeeping in the yurta does not demand the time and strength or the attention to a multiplicity of details that home-making in most other countries of the world demands of women.

The yurta, constructed as it is, so that an entire encampment can be packed up ready to be moved on oxcarts in an hour and set up again in the same time, is a home containing only the essentials. It does not take very long to clean out the brazier every morning and start a fresh fire, shake the rugs, fold up the furs on which the family has slept on the ground during the night, and make the place neat. The food of the plains people is simple and does not take very long to prepare. In summer they live almost entirely on the milk of goats, sheep, cows, mares, and camels, and the cheese made from it.

The cheese is simple of manufacture. Crude cheeses of the five kinds of milk are made in the same way. The milk is heated in an iron pot over an argol fire until the curd separates from the water. The curd is taken out, put in a cloth, and pressed between stones. When the water is all pressed out the cheese is moulded into cakes and laid in the sun to dry. Cheese which is to be stored for winter use is dried until very hard. It is eaten melted in hot tea, and is very nourishing.

Cream cheese is made by heating whole milk until the cream rises to the top and thickens. This is skimmed off and made into soft cakes. Cream cheese cannot be stored, but must be eaten at once. Cheese made from mare's milk has a sourish taste. Mare's milk will not make butter. The Mongols use cow's milk only for making it. In the summer, when milk is abundant, butter is put up for the winter.

It is made in the following way. The cream is skimmed from milk and shaken in a skin churn until butter forms. The butter is put in a pot over the fire and melted, then boiled a long time until it is very clear. After that it is put away in stone jars for winter. No salt is added. Butter prepared in this way will keep for many months without going rancid, but it must be boiled until it is transparently clear.

Mare's milk is made into "kumiss" in every part of Mongolia, and is one of the principal drinks of the country. It not only quenches thirst, but it satisfies hunger. When I have a long hard day of perhaps more than a hundred miles in the saddle, I find it wisest to follow the Mongolian's example and nourish my body only with mare's milk. Kumiss is made by hanging mare's milk in rawhide bags and leaving it in the sun for several days. It should be stirred two or three times each day.

It is the custom all over Mongolia for the head woman of the family to offer milk to the gods every day. She stands in front of the encampment with a basin of milk and a dipper. With the dipper she throws the milk in every direction, turning first east, then north, then west, then south.

In summer it is not customary to kill a sheep except when a large enough party are gathered together to eat it all at one time, because before the first of September meat in Mongolia spoils overnight. In winter, when meat can be kept frozen, cattle as well as sheep are killed. The meat is cut in strips and hung up in a yurta where there is no fire so that it will freeze.

The Mongolian religion forbids the taking of the lives of animals, but since the climate is so bitterly cold that it seems to make the eating of meat a necessity, lama priests and lay folk all eat it. The only people who can kill are those who are specially appointed by the temple to do so. Even in wintry days when badly in need of meat, a family has to wait until a properly authorized person can get through to the camp and kill an animal for its use.

The Mongolian people use brick tea imported from China. "Tut, tut, tut," is the early morning

sound in every Mongolian yurta over the land — the
pounding of brick tea on the stone mortar, ready for
the day's use. The Mongols make tea in the following
manner. A big handful of tea is put in an iron caul-
dron with milk, a handful of salt, and a lump of
butter. The mixture is stirred and tossed high with
a dipper as it is boiled, so that the salt, tea, and milk
are well compounded. When I first went to Mongolia
my palate rebelled against saline tea, but after I had
drunk it for several weeks I cultivated an appetite
for it. Now I accept it in tents and palaces with en-
thusiastic relish. It is a good food when one is
hungry and tired, and is easily digested.

The Mongol makes tea with salt, but cooks mutton
and beef without it. This is a peculiarity which one
has to get used to also.

All the clothes worn in Mongolia are made by the
women, from fur coats to fine embroidered tobacco
pouches. Women also make the boots. Mongolian
men and women both like their riding boots with
original and beautiful designs in colored leather
either hammered into them or sewn on. For use in
the house the women make attractive low slippers
which they embroider in bright colors.

A good many of the women are absolute rulers in
their yurtas. They know and keep track of every
animal in every flock and herd, and will not permit
the men of their family to sell or trade them without
their consent. Often when I have wanted to buy a
good horse of a man he has asked me to wait until
he has obtained the consent of his wife. As a rule
I find such families very prosperous, because women

seem to be better able than men to attend to the small things that build a fortune. They check waste, and nurse sick animals or weak lambs and calves and foals, more wisely than men.

Compared to those of the West, the morals of the Mongolian women are, to put it mildly, lax. There has never been a double-standard system in Mongolia. The Mongolian woman is not the property of her husband, but a free and independent personality who can and does do exactly as she pleases. She takes the passing lama or friendly traveler as lover without shame or censure. This is and has been a bad thing for the race, because it has caused disease to be spread through Mongolia and made the birth rate very low.

Children are prized and welcomed everywhere in Mongolia. There is no baby born that goes looking for a home. It is not a disgrace if a girl has a child before marriage; in such a case she puts up her hair on the day her child is born, and after this wears a married woman's headdress. This is spoken of as "marriage at home."

Mongolian families are very small, often childless; seldom with more than one or two children; in a few, very rare, instances, as many as five. The Mongolian woman, when she does bear a child, seems to have little difficulty. A doctor is never called in. Another woman of the family takes care of her and the child. When the baby is three or four days old, friends come with charms for it — brass coins, old bronze figures, little idols, and various tiny trinkets which they put on a string tied around the baby's neck for

it to play with. Then there is a little feast, and the
child is wrapped up in a new quilt specially made for
it. The mother wraps the child up in the presence
of all the guests.

The baby cannot be given a name except by an
incarnate lama or a Living Buddha. Sometimes it
has only a pet name until it is three or four years old.
Mongol people use no family name. They are simply
known by the name given them by the Living Buddha
or incarnate lama. Children of either sex are equally
welcomed and treated affectionately. All children are
loved by everybody in Mongolia. No child is or-
phaned for many hours. Any number of homes are
open to it.

The education of a Mongolian child is, according
to the Western idea, usually nil, for very few children
receive any book learning. Perhaps this is not so
necessary to the Mongolian child as it is to the European and the American. Teachers, however, are to
be found, and are sometimes called by an important
family father who wants his child to read and write
Mongolian.

The Mongol is not troubled by dialects. A person
from one part of the country has no difficulty in
understanding a person from another part: the Mongols have roamed too freely on horseback to develop
dialects. The written language has an alphabet. It is
written perpendicularly in lines from left to right.

The eldest son in every family goes to the lama
temple as a priest. There he learns the religious
language — Tibetan. He can repeat a great many
prayers in this language — often without under-

standing a single one of the sounds he makes. He seldom learns to use Tibetan so that he could talk with Tibetan people.

The Mongolian child grows up near to nature and learns by daily experience, and from the book of the world which is spread before him, a great deal that is denied to children who live in cities. He knows the ways of birds and squirrels and antelopes and wolves, of the swallow that builds on the top of the yurta, as well as the habits of the horses he rides from the age of five. The Mongol boy or girl knows when very young how to get about in his or her own country and what is necessary to do under all circumstances.

Any child of ten in Mongolia could fend for himself prudently and capably. I have seen boys and girls of six or seven pick up a stick and dash out fearlessly when they have sighted a wolf menacing the sheep herd — and have seen the wolf slink away, frightened by the bold manner and voice of the child.

The Mongol in travel takes little with him besides the horse he rides. It is my habit to travel through the country in this same way. Mongolian hospitality extends a cordial welcome to any guest who has need of food or shelter. The folk in every Mongolian encampment know that all of them will desire the same courtesy the day when they also have to take a journey. People who live as the nomad Mongol lives, in a free open country, are folk of simple, kindly heart, who share graciously whatever they possess.

So, when night comes, the traveler rides up to an encampment. It is the custom, if the people have not seen his arrival, to shout out asking them to call off their dogs. Then someone comes out, calls away the dogs, and waits by the hitching place until the visitor has dismounted.

When two people meet in Mongolia they do not shake hands as in Western countries. Instead, each takes out his or her snuffbox. They exchange bottles, and raise them to their noses, but seldom take out the stoppers and help themselves to snuff. They simply lower them again and, holding the hands close together, give them back, at the same time exchanging such greetings as "Have you come in peace?" — "I have come in peace — does your encampment dwell in peace?" After this they walk together to the entrance of the guest tent.

A guest, according to custom, does not take his riding whip into the tent of his host, but lays it on the top of the yurta as he passes in. He also draws his knife sheath from his girdle and lets it hang free on the chains dangling about his knees — a sign that he is a peaceful friend. Inside the tent, the host or hostess presses the visitor to accept the highest seat of honor, that nearest the family altar. Here a cushion on which to sit, and one propped up on which to rest the back, have been placed.

A polite Mongol guest does not thrust his feet toward the fire — to do so is to insult the family hearth; it would be equivalent to spitting in the face of one's host in a Western country. He sits with his feet folded back under him.

When the guest has been comfortably seated, tea, which is always kept hot and ready for guests in Mongol yurtas, is served to him, no matter what hour of the day or night he has called. Then the family gather around and ask him questions about his herds, his flocks, and concerning the water where his family are encamped, give information about their own well-being, and laugh and joke concerning innumerable things until the evening meal has been cooked. This is milk and cheese or mutton, and is served in just as great abundance as the family can afford. If, for any reason, the host wishes to show his guest that he has honored him by his visit, a bowl of milk is presented to him on a white silk scarf.

The long silk scarf, of richness in accord with wealth, plays a large part in the etiquette of the Mongolian people. At the New Year everyone must go and call on relatives and friends, carrying a silk scarf which should be presented on both hands outspread and received with both hands. If friends or relatives live far away, one member of the family is sent with scarves from all the others, carrying greetings. Children, however, are usually sent small presents wrapped up in tiny scarves.

If a passing traveler, stopping the night in an encampment, happens to be going to the locality of friends or relatives of his host, it is polite to send a silk scarf by him, with wishes for peace and happiness.

If anyone of the Mongol's acquaintance is elevated to a high position, it is a politeness to send a silk scarf with congratulations. Silk scarves are always sent to the Living Buddha, to lamas, or to a doctor when making a request for help in sickness.

But to return to the procedure when a guest stops at an encampment. After the evening meal is served all join in making the time jolly. Everyone tells humorous stories of his or her adventures or some interesting incident that has happened in the herds. Perhaps there is music. The Mongols are very fond of music — singing, the flute, or a stringed instrument which is something like the violin.

Often Mongols have very pleasing singing voices. They have no written music or set song, but sing historic folk tales — not all ancient tales, for every generation adds to history here. I have spent many happy evenings listening to the combined harmony of flute, violin, and voice.

Everyone in Mongolia retires at an early hour. Wealthy families always have a guest tent ready for any passing traveler, furnished with everything one needs. Families that are not well off give the guest the best place in their own sleeping quarters — the place farthest from the door and nearest the altar on which stand the images of the gods.

All things in Mongolia have a simple order. In undressing, the Mongol people have an etiquette in regard to the placing of clothes. All garments worn below the waist must be placed below the feet; all garments worn above the waist must be laid above the head. All Mongols are modest, and in families that do not possess private sleeping tents people undress under their sleeping rugs.

The guest is provided with furs to keep warm at

night and tucked in snugly by the host. Then the mother of the family banks the fire. If it is winter, the top flat of the yurta is drawn nearly shut and a rug is dropped over the door to keep out the wind. In the morning the guest must be given a good meal and plenty of hot tea before going on. Then his horse, which has been turned out to graze with his host's horses, is caught, bridled and saddled, and the guest takes his departure, riding on across country until he has need of another meal or another night's shelter. To offer to pay a host is an insult; payment is in like hospitality when a traveler passes one's own home.

Horses in Mongolia always turn in to every encampment if given a free rein. The traveler making a leisurely progress across country usually does stop at every encampment for a word or two with the people and a cup of tea. Mongol encampments are not very close together, and the people of the yurta are always glad for a word, as they have no newspapers or postal service. It is the traveler who brings them news from friends and neighbors.

In a yurta where there is a sick person a rope is fastened to the left side of the yurta door with one end tied to a stick and driven into the ground on the east side of the tent. A stranger coming to the yurta knows that there is a sick person within and so will not enter the tent. Time of sickness is the only time when a visitor cannot expect genial hospitality.

It is the habit in Mongolia, when one meets a fellow man, woman, or child on horseback, to draw rein and exchange friendly conversation concerning health and peace, the flocks, what the weather has been, where each is going or coming from. People here do not wait for introductions, but take each other on friendly trust. Two men going the same way across country fall in together, riding their horses stride for stride, although they may never have seen each other before their roads met. In traveling in Mongolia, we go straight across country over the rolling green turf.

There are no broken roads; we ride in the direction of the place we seek and ask at yurtas for information concerning the whereabouts of the nomad encampments of friends. It is a wonderful feeling to gallop thus ever toward the horizon across the thick green turf on an unshod horse with the undulating plain stretching away into the dim purple distance, then over a rise of hill to come on to a cluster of white tents nestling cosily near a watering place.

One morning in June I met a ragged old woman, with a twig basket strapped on her back and a twig shovel in her hand, gathering argol — the dried dropping of animals which is the only fuel in Mongolia except in the north and northeast, where there is luxuriant forest supplying fuel. Great piles of argol are stacked by every encampment or palace ready for use. In autumn enough for the winter must be collected before the snow comes. The winter supply is sealed over with wet cow dung to make it waterproof. Argol burns without odor and makes a clean, quick, hot fire with little smoke. But the gathering of argol is the meanest task in Mongolia. It is a job which must be done on foot in a land where folk prefer never to work except from the saddle.

I was seated on a splendid horse and I felt sorry for the poor old woman with the dirty heavy basket of dung on her back. Pitying her, I thought of her as a peasant serf and remembered that in Mongolia every commoner must kneel when a noble passes, that a month of each commoner's labor belongs to the ruler of his state if the ruler desires it, and that at the end of every summer a portion of all argol gathered, as well as a percentage of all herds and flocks and their by-products, must be given to the monarch for his use.

But the old woman straightened her back from her work and stood independent and haughty as a queen as she spoke to me: "You are a foreigner — whence have you come? Has your journey been in peace?"

When I had answered her briefly she said with pity: "How sad for you that you are not born a Mongol — but how fortunate you are that you have found your way to Mongolia before you died!"

Her dirty twig shovel was a queen's sceptre as she waved it in a circle which encompassed the flower-jeweled plain fragrant with the spicy perfume of wild carnations; the hundreds of graceful antelopes that fed on the tender grass; a pair of bobbed white-tail gazelles with a pretty fawn between them; dozens of hares (that were exact replicas of the Easter bunnies in Swedish shop windows at Easter times) hopping happily about; grey field mice peacefully sunning themselves by their burrows with no fear of humans;

the thrushes and song sparrows trilling rhapsodies of delight; and a lark that hung suspended in mid-heaven, above the nest where his mate brooded, pouring forth a crystal shower of melody.

As I rode on I noticed, as I had never noticed before, how serenely happy and peacefully contented are all the folk I have met in Mongolia, and how laughter rings from even the poorest yurta.

III

LAMAISM

I WRITE this chapter at evening time, by candlelight, seated on the floor in a white felt yurta. I am a guest in the encampment of a Mongolian family whom I have known for many years. My yurta is next in line above the "god's tent": my low writing table vibrates with the throb of moaning lama drums. Above the drums I hear the alto chant of lama priests repeating Tibetan prayers.

Chactar, my old friend, has not been well for many months. Priests have been called from a temple to hold a week of special prayer for his health. Chactar himself is a lama priest. So are his nephew and his grandnephew. The first-born sons of three generations! Three males from a family that numbers but five males in all: that leaves one grown man and one small boy of three summers to fulfill the material duties of life. And this is not an unusually devout family. Most of the families of my acquaintance show a similar percentage of males in the priesthood.

An alarming percentage of the male population of Mongolia are lama priests. Custom requires that every first-born son shall be given to the priesthood, and as many more sons thereafter as possible. This is a great drain on the family, for it leaves a very small proportion to carry on the work of caring for the herds and the flocks; but the more lama priests given by each family, the greater the virtue of that family. According to the religion which holds Mongolia in an iron grip, health, wealth, and happiness are dependent upon the dedication of many sons to the temple.

By strict regulations, lama priests are forbidden to marry. This has played an important part in the depopulation of the country, although not all priests observe this order.

Demp-si, the lama priest who is elder brother of the head of this family, was married a few months ago with much ceremony. Demp-si has always liked the ladies. His fondness for them has led him in past years to give away as gifts some of the best horses from the family herds, in addition to many cows, goats, sheep, felt, and other trifles. The family have found this continuous drain an annoyance, so in council they decided that the best solution was for Demp-si to marry. He is married now to a very pretty girl, who seems a practical, sensible woman, likely to keep him in order.

Buddhism came into Mongolia through the conversion of the wife of Kublai Khan by a priest from Tibet. The Mongols look upon Tibet as their spiritual home. When traveling through Mongolia I continually come upon pilgrims either en route to Tibet or returning from there. Lamaism is a compound of black magic, nature worship, and Buddhism. It is the national religion of Mongolia, and numbers among its adherents almost the entire population. Lama temples dot the entire country from the borders of Russia to China. The maintenance of these

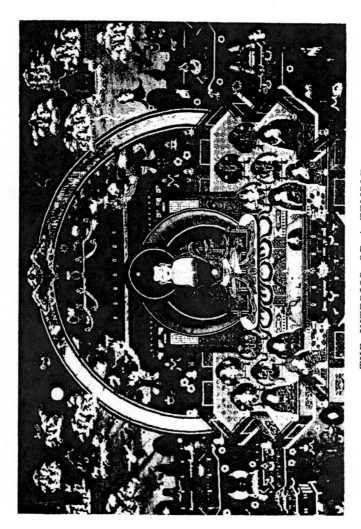

THE INTERIOR OF A TEMPLE

lamasseries is a heavy tax on Mongolia. It is not only the building, furnishing, and keeping in repair of the temples that is expensive, but more than one third of the population of Mongolia is drawn into them as lama priests and must be supported by the lay population.

Lamasseries are the only religious buildings in Mongolia, except for a few Christian mission houses. Some of the lamasseries number their inmates by the thousand. Others have only a resident population of below a hundred, with a number of adherent priests who spend a part of the year in their homes in the country.

Every state in Mongolia has a large lamassery in which state services are held. Many other lamasseries have been founded and endowed by wealthy families. In such cases a son of the family, in inherited succession, is the abbot; the lower lamas are drawn from the family's friends and neighbors.

Gifts from pilgrims and devout worshipers form a portion of the lamassery income. Many lamasseries also make money in trade. Even the smallest temple in Mongolia has at least one horse herd.

In the summer time, if one travels from temple to temple, one comes upon horse fairs continually. At these fairs a lucrative business is done by the priests.

The lamasseries in Mongolia are all either of the Manchurian type of architecture or copies of the Tibetan temples. They are built by imported labor, usually Chinese, for the Mongols are not builders and have never even tried to learn anything about masonry.

Sites for temples are chosen to command the finest possible outlook over the surrounding country. If possible, the temple faces the east, so that it may receive the first rays of the rising sun. It is considered unlucky for a monastery to face a running stream, for then all virtue might be drained from it. It is considered a good omen for the lamassery to have its back against a rock or a hillside.

When a site has been selected, there is an elaborate consecration ceremony. The local astrologer sets the auspicious day for this: prayers are recited and the gods are invited to extend their protection. On the day that building operations are commenced there is a still more elaborate ceremony. Charms, relics, and copies of sacred books are placed under the foundations.

The monasteries really are an imposing and beautiful sight, standing as they do on the rolling green plateau. They are two or three stories in height. The ground floor is devoted to the central hall of worship, sometimes with small chapels on either side of it. The storerooms are usually to the back. The floor above this is usually a granary or larder.

In the main building are the living quarters of the chief lamas. Smaller buildings cluster round the central building. These sometimes make the lamassery appear a good-sized village. The lesser lamas are housed in these outbuildings.

In front of the main doors of the temple there is always a large courtyard for outdoor ceremonies and celebrations during the summer months.

A prayer wheel is placed on either side of the entrance. These prayer wheels are sometimes of considerable size — eight or nine feet in height, and seven in diameter. They are turned by a crank and fitted with a bell that rings at each complete revolution. I have two beautiful big bronze prayer wheels as curios in my home in Kalgan.

Around the outer wall of the lamassery, which is usually square, there are placed one hundred and eight prayer wheels. These are sheltered from the weather by the overhanging eaves, and are at a convenient height from the ground so that pious people may perform a circle of prayer round the temple, revolving each wheel, in order to win the favor of Heaven.

The interior decorations of a temple depend on the wealth of an institution. In Mongolia the temples are kept in excellent repair, in sharp contrast to the decaying temples of China. The gods are always well dusted and the ornaments bright, even if of poor material. If the lamassery is rich, the streamers that hang from the ceiling are of beautiful brocade, and the religious banners depicting the Buddhas, the saints, the deified demons, and the evil spirits are of lovely workmanship.

One usually finds an image of Buddha or some other famous saint on the main altar, flanked on either side by minor deities. The altar vessels, lamps, and holy-water bowls are of gold or silver, according to the wealth of the place. The seats of the lamas are just bare boards, if the lamassery is poor; covered with rich silk cushions with silken canopies suspended over them, if it is prosperous.

Often beautiful old rugs lie on the floor. Dimly burning butter lamps light the altars.

All the images are draped with silk scarfs of honor. Sometimes the idols are clothed in brocade. In addition to the large images on the main altar there are many small images in niches round the central throne and on the shrines in the side temples. Sometimes these tiny idols are of pure gold — the gift of pious pilgrims. The bases of some images are filled with crushed gems — crushed so that the lamas may not be tempted to steal them. Prayers are also often put in the base of an idol. Canopies of silk fashioned of gorgeous material often hang over the idols.

The walls of the temples are decorated with pictures painted in bright colors by artistic lamas. There is always one depicting the region of the gods. This is represented as a land filled with all the things that the heart of man can desire — fine felt yurtas, spirited horses, cows with full udders, sheep with wool hanging heavy on them; the gods supplied with food which comes to them without care or trouble, and with sparkling drinks with which to quench their thirst. Goddesses clothed in gorgeous raiment are always there to keep them company.

The next picture shows the realm of demigods. This is a world of ghosts, or spirits doomed to live for a few hundred years in the land of spectres. These spirits are shown as naked, with hideous bodies and long thin necks. They are supposed to be people who when on earth were gluttonous, miserly, or avaricious. All the good things of life are displayed in abundance on a table within their reach, but fate punishes them: whatever food or drink they consume is immediately changed into sharp blades that cut their insides, or liquid fire that burns them. In this kingdom there is always a queen with five hundred lovely phantom children at her feet — just beyond her reach.

Above this land of torment there is a god sprinkling the unfortunate people with holy water to assuage their suffering. The god of wisdom is always included in this picture, and Buddha is near at hand to liberate souls who have been purified by punishment.

Then there is usually a picture painted on a wall to the left of the realm of the gods, and this is the world of mankind. In it officials and their servants are busy with state business. Lamas are seated in deep meditation. Herdsmen and their wives and children are contentedly busy with the usual domestic tasks of life. This is a happy picture. Below it is another picture divided into two parts, representing grotesque animals, some who live in the water and some who live above it. Such human beings as have sinned through stupidity are reborn into this realm. They must go through a cycle of life as animals who suffer cruelties at the hands of humans.

But the artists seem most facile with the brush in the depiction of hells. These are, according to Lamaism, of sixteen different kinds — eight cold and eight hot. Each is presided over by a king. The pictures show the tongues of slanderers enlarged with heated irons. Men who have made sharp bargains have their flesh crushed between white-hot plates. Persons who have been cruel to animals are shown suffering in the cold hall, where their flesh and skin is made to crack and split by exposure until their bodies are masses of festering sores. These sores are not allowed to heal, but are picked by birds with beaks of iron. The tortures are all carried out by spirits — animal-headed, with human bodies.

A wealthy lamassery, such as has the ruler of a state as its patron, is a gorgeous sight when a service is in progress and when the priests in gold or crimson robes of beautiful material fill the richly furnished temple.

The outside of a Mongolian temple, if it is copied from the Tibetan, is kept freshly whitewashed. If of the Manchu style of architecture, the mosaic under the eaves and the heavy round wooden pillars furnish color in contrast to the stone of the buildings. In the Tibetan form of temple, which is really much more often seen than the Manchu, banners of black haircloth striped with white flutter from raised poles about the monastery to frighten away evil spirits.

Every monastery has a stupa or tope erected round it, in which are deposited relics, sacred books, and various precious things. Each one has five divisions, representing the five elements — metal, wood, water, fire, and earth. The stupa is erected usually in memory of a saint, a lama, or some very much beloved member of a family. Those built by wealthy people often have the three upper elements covered with gold leaf. The others are carefully whitewashed.

Some distance from the temple there is always a circle defining the border of the holy ground. This circle is made by heaps of stones at intervals, perhaps ten inches apart. Priests walk round these stones chanting prayers, or sometimes in penance for some sin that they have committed.

Women may go into a temple to pray in the daytime, but after sunset no woman may pass beyond the circle of stones, or tarry therein.

Children destined for the religious life are sent to the temple any time up to the eighth year. I have often seen children as young as two or three already inmates of a monastery. According to the regulations, a child entered for the priesthood should not have any physical blemish. There is no real medical examination, as we understand it, but it is called such in the book of rules. It simply means that a child with bodily disfigurement or an impediment of speech is not considered a suitable candidate.

In certain monasteries only novices from good families are admitted — that is, families whose reputation has been excellent for generations.

The child, after he has been accepted by the monastery, is handed over to the care of a senior priest who is held responsible for the education, discipline, and morals of his pupil. If possible, a senior priest who is a relative of the child is selected; but if this cannot be arranged, the matter is decided by consulting the child's horoscope. The teacher of a boy is presented with gifts by the child's parents at the time that he is taken over; these vary in accordance with the wealth of the family.

After a short period the senior priest takes his

pupil before the assembled priests of the monastery and seeks their sanction for his protégé to enter the order. The boy is now classed as a novice — probationer. After this, if he is small, he has one guardian who looks after his food and material needs, and another who teaches him his religious texts. In return for his tutor's care he must perform for them such menial services as he is able. When the boy has learned a certain number of Tibetan prayers by rote, none of which he understands, as Tibetan is not his native language, he is sent up for examination before the priests again. If he repeats smoothly and well what he is supposed to know, he moves up one step further. He is now supposed to be ready for higher education.

The tutor approaches the abbot of the monastery about this, sending in to him at the same time as valuable gifts as the boy's parents can afford to make. Provided all things are in order, the names of the pupil and his tutor are now entered in a higher register. Opposite their names their thumb impressions are put, and below the thumb impressions the seals of two citizens who vouch for them.

Until now the budding lama has worn his ordinary lay clothes. During the ceremony of entrance upon his higher education he has been dressed in all the finery that he could possibly afford — the most gorgeous robes of a layman; but at the end of the ceremony he is stripped of all his gay raiment and clad in the sombre attire of a priest, and a scarf is knotted about his throat. This signifies his renunciation of all material things and his entry into the serious world of religion. Many monks never pass beyond this stage, either because they do not have the necessary funds or because they are too dull to learn any more prayers. In the case of a rich student, bribery often makes up for dullness.

Every monastery has hostels in which the student monks reside. Usually in these hostels messes of four or five eat together. Accommodation depends entirely upon wealth and rank. Four, five, or even six poor monks may have to share a single room, while a lad from a wealthy family will have a private room all to himself, nicely furnished. Of course, monks who have risen through examination to a high place each have a private apartment. The rooms of wealthy people are richly furnished; the rooms of poor people have only a small shrine, a blanket, and the floor, which serves as a seat by day and a bed by night.

Once a monk has donned his priestly robes and equipment he must dress in them; he cannot again garb himself in lay clothes. These consist of a voluminous skirt, a sleeveless waistcoat, a large serge scarf for covering the shoulders, and a cap. The color is either crimson or yellow, depending upon the sect of Lamaism the temple belongs to. Each priest also wears a rosary.

The next step is for the novice to apply to the abbot for permission to take part in the temple services. He likewise accompanies his request with gifts according to his means. If his prayer is granted, a favorable day is fixed for the ceremony. Early in the morning a brother priest shaves his head, leaving

only a small tuft of hair on the top of the skull. At
the hour of service in the temple, led by his tutor, he
presents himself clad in beggar's rags to the assembled monks and says that he accepts the holy priesthood as his career by his own choice. The head lama
of the monastery then cuts off the remaining tufts
of hair.

Now the applicant is given a religious name by
which he is henceforth known. The ceremony is
concluded by the repetition of the formula, "I take
refuge in Buddha, in the law, and in the priesthood."

The next celebration of service is called the ceremony of marriage with the Church. The young
priest enters the temple holding a bundle of incense
sticks. He is led by a monk who is called the "companion of the bride." The young priest places his
incense sticks before the altar, lights them, and
prostrates himself, promising never to make an
earthly marriage but to live in union with religion.

He takes his seat in an appointed place and is instructed in the rules and conduct of religious services.
He is taught how a priest should sit, how he should
hold his hands, how he should walk, and all the
etiquette of behavior in a temple.

From this time on the novitiate enjoys many of
the privileges of a fully ordained monk. After three
or four years, according to his progress in his studies,
he is given better quarters in his hostel, regardless
of how thin his purse may be. Now he must mem-
orize volume after volume of sacred books. If he
slackens in his work his tutor does not hesitate to
inflict corporal punishment, for should he fail in his

examination the tutor is in danger of a beating himself by order of the higher priests.

Public debates are a favorite method of testing the knowledge of a novitiate priest. These take on something of the color of a festival. Thrones are built in the temple garden for the abbot and other high lamas who may be present. One student takes his stand before the throne and acts as questioner. His opponent sits before him. Only student monks of the same grade may dispute together. The other monks gather around in a circle and listen to the debate.

From now on the novice may continue to pass periodical examinations, take part in public disputations, and commit books to memory as long as he cares to do so. It takes twelve years or more for a boy to become a full-fledged lama. No monk can reach this rank before the age of twenty, and in actual practice few ever attain it before forty. After this he has an opportunity to study metaphysics and the more abstruse works of Tibetan religious literature. Some novices take up the study of magic and leave their monastery with a degree which authorizes them to practise this art publicly. Others feel inclined toward care of the sick and learn how to treat illnesses according to the weird and wonderful lama theories. A few of these are really wise in the use of herbs and are very successful in treating diseases with the healing roots and leaves that they gather from the surrounding country.

The treatment of the sick, whether by magic or weird prayer theory or herbs, is the most lucrative

profession inside the priesthood. In time of bad
health people will part with all their wealth to be
restored to normal physical condition again. Un-
scrupulous priests take advantage of this: often after
an epidemic all the good horses, camels, cattle, sheep,
and goats from the surrounding families are the
property either of a lamassery or of individual lamas.

Last year when in Sinkiang on Dr. Hedin's expedition I had with me a young Mongol, named
Batu, who is a member of a family I have known
for thirty years. They have always been prudent,
thrifty people possessed of extensive herds and
flocks. Batu and I returned to his home state together. When we were about ten miles from the
well where he expected to find his family camped
for the summer grazing we saw a man riding furiously
along the ridge of a hill. As he came near, Batu
exclaimed, "That is one of our horses — it is ridden
by my cousin."

He signaled to the rider and we both went to meet
him. It was Batu's cousin on the way to a lamassery
to fetch the priests. Batu's family were dying of
typhus. He explained that Batu's mother and his
elder brother, head of the family, were dangerously
sick. We had planned that after a few days' visit
at Batu's home he should accompany me to the
neighboring state of Sunit, where I had an important
errand. The sickness in his home changed our plans.
After giving him all the advice I could about how to
care for typhus patients, I went on and left him busy
with his people.

Two months later, when I had left Sunit and gone

on into another state, Batu rode into the camp where I was a guest. He came for help. His mother, brother, and eleven others of the family were dead. He was now head man of the family, with all the burden of its maintenance on his shoulders — and the family herds and flocks were held by lama priests in return for care of the sick and the dead.

When their course of study is finished at the temple, some lamas return to their families and reside with them. A few refuse to dwell in a lamassery again; but the usual practice is for priests living with their relatives to return to the temple for a few weeks every year.

Priests who live at home often work as hard as the lay folk in the family. They share in the care of the herds and flocks, or assist in the taking down and putting up of yurtas when the camp moves, as well as guide their kin in religious matters.

Many pious lamas go on long pilgrimages to the temples of Tibet or to Wu-Tai-Shan in Shansi. They must walk the entire way and carry their possessions on their back. A lama who has shown such piety is regarded as a very holy man: Mongol folk consider it a hard penance both to walk and to leave the homeland.

There is a close union between the lamasseries and the people. That is easily understood seeing that each first-born son goes into a temple. A religion which has power to draw every first-born son from a people whose birth rate is so low has a strangle hold. Most Mongols refer every important matter to a lamassery for decision. Few will set out on a journey

until a lama has stated that the selected day is
auspicious.

Each temple has the following organization. At
the head there is an abbot and an incarnate lama —
that is, a lama in whose body dwells the spirit of a
Buddhist saint. Below these two heads comes the
"Big Lama," who is in charge of the ritual of the
monastery services. Below him are the provost mar-
shals, two or three according to the size of the monastery. These are responsible for the maintenance of
order. As sign of their authority they carry rawhide
whips.

Next in rank comes the treasurer, who supervises
the collection of revenues and administers expend-
itures; then monks who are responsible for the safe
custody of the clothing, furniture, carpets, tables,
implements, and banners used in the services. Below
these are the teachers, then the senior monks; below
them, junior monks who fill the offices of water
carriers and tea offerers to their seniors during the
services. Lastly, there are officers who have no duties
inside the monastery in connection with the religious
services, but who receive guests, travel through the
country collecting gifts from the people for the
monastery, or even barter and trade to increase
the temple funds.

When an incarnate lama dies, the spirit of the saint
that has dwelt in him enters the body of a child who
is born at the instant the lama dies. After the death,
a deputation consisting of other incarnate lamas and
learned lamas of rank search for the child in whom

this spirit has been reborn. They are guided by the advice of astrologers. Then they proceed to the district indicated. Here the committee inquire for any newborn child whose entrance into the world has been marked by such omens as showers of shooting stars or the herds showing signs of unusual restlessness. Four or five such children may be discovered; their names are all written down.

Then, when the children are a few months old, the priests come again to each yurta where there is such a baby and lay before him articles that belonged to the dead lama. If a child turns away from these things, then the lamas go on to the next baby. And so on until they find one that greets them with pleasure. This they think is a sign that the incarnate saint has recognized his own possessions. One meets such committees continually in Mongolia. I have talked with them many times. Their methods have not changed in the least since I first came to Mongolia.

The general routine life of a lama in a temple is as follows. He is awakened in the morning within a half-hour of the commencement of the daybreak service by the beating of a large gong, followed by blasts from a conch-shell trumpet. This is the signal for him to rise and wash his hands and face. He does not often wash in winter; dirt is warm, and the lamas do not like cold. After the perfunctory washing parade, the monks repair to the temple hall, where they seat themselves in their places according to their rank and seniority.

First a short silence is observed by all the monks,

a breach of which is punished by the provost's whip. Then the lamas chant their prayers in unison. This is followed by a lecture on morals and deportment. Then novices serve the seated lamas with cups of Mongolian tea and bowls of food. In wealthy temples the tea is poured from beautiful pots of copper with heavy silver ornamentation.

After the tea special services are performed. These may be for the repose of the soul of a deceased person, for recovery from sickness, or as penance for committed sins — any of the many things for which the intervention of the priests is required and paid for. A proverb says, "There is no approach to God unless a lama leads the way." The monks are now supposed to return to their cubicles for private devotions.

In mid-morning another service of about an hour is held in the temple. After this the novices receive instruction. Then at noon there is chanting of prayers, after which tea and food is served. In mid-afternoon there is another service, following which the novices are given more instruction and the elder monks practise playing the musical instruments with which evil spirits are chased away. The last celebration of the day is just before sunset. Then the students repeat to their teachers the lessons they have learned during the day, and the senior monks attend to private affairs. Shortly after this the bell of retirement sounds.

Lama priests are supposed to lead celibate lives. They take vows by which they promise to do so; but they enter the monasteries when they are very young and when they do not understand these vows. They are human men with the passions of other men: very few of them are able to abstain from women. The women of Mongolia revere the priests, so temptation is before them constantly. The priests live with many kinds of women and help to spread horrible diseases throughout Mongolia.

Very few priests stay in their temples the entire year. They return to their homes or travel wherever they are needed, to read prayers for the sick, dispose of the dead, decide on a marriage day, select a new pitch for an encampment, or execute any of the various errands to collect funds for the lamassery which they frequently undertake. They travel on horseback, as everyone does in Mongolia, and usually sleep in a different tent each night. The Mongolian birth rate is very low because of the prevalence of syphilis and other diseases spread in this way.

When a person dies in Mongolia the lamas are sent for immediately. They read prayers first for the repose of the dead spirit. Then a priest versed in black magic selects a suitable place to lay the body. The priests measure a plot with a rope and place the body there entirely nude. The corpse is covered with a white cloth. The lamas repeat prayers over it and it is left for three days.

During these three days the lamas feast in a yurta prepared for them by the deceased's relatives, reading prayers and holding services for the benefit of the spirit. No one goes near the place where the body has been left until the morning of the third day.

Then, if the eagles and the wolves have devoured it, the Mongols are satisfied that the spirit has passed into Heaven. They consider that a human being was good or bad according to the quickness or slowness with which the remains of the earthly body disappear.

This is a gruesome practice which made horrible the territory just outside the city of Urga. Urga is the only place in Mongolia where a multitude of Mongols live close together. But no encampment is safe from the possibility that one of the family dogs may come in dragging a human leg or arm. Thirty-five years in Mongolia has not inured me to this. I shudder with horror every time it happens.

There are Mongols also who cannot bring themselves to lay their beloved dead out for the wolves to devour or dogs to tear to pieces. Some few families burn their corpses and send the ashes to repose in a holy place such as a niche in a Tibetan temple or the temple of Wu-Tai-Shan.

Lama priests use the bones of human bodies in various ways. After animals have devoured the flesh of a dead body, lamas gather up the bones that are left. Skull bones are used to make rosary beads. A lama rosary consists of one hundred and eight beads, each cut from a different skull. The priests use these beads to count off as they say their prayers. The lamas also use human skulls as drinking cups. The bones are thoroughly dried and cleaned; then a silversmith lines them with silver. Such cups are not used every day, but on special holy occasions.

Human bones are used to make instruments for

driving away devils. The most common are trumpets made from the thigh bones of maidens and drums made from a young girl's and a young boy's skull. To make the drums the top of each cranium is cut off even and the two craniums are placed with their backs together. Then skin is stretched tightly over them. The drums are painted green and decorated with bright ribbons embroidered with the eight emblems of lamassery sacrifice. Two leather thongs hang down from each drum, each with a clapper on the end. When the priest reads prayers against the devil he completes the anti-devil charm by twisting the drum in his hand so that the clappers rap a sharp staccato.

In localities where things constantly go wrong — where wells dry up, cattle die of rinderpest, wolves destroy a sheep flock, or a woman deserts her husband — Mongols believe that a devil is abroad. So they call upon the local lamassery to help rid their territory of this evil. Lamas and laymen on horseback form a circle all about the land where there has been trouble. Armed with devil drums and prayer banners, they gallop in, driving everything before them, until their horses' heads make a closed circle.

Then the priests read prayers denouncing the evil devil who, although invisible in the eyes of humans, must certainly be captive within the wall made by the horses' forelegs. When the devil has been sufficiently cursed they build a jail of stones foursquare and shut him inside. This they seal up tightly. Then they go back to their encampments assured that now all will be well so long as the prison remains tightly sealed.

As a common-sense precaution a series of devil dances are held every summer at each lamassery. Dressed in grotesque costumes with ugly false animal heads, the lama priests caper about in ugly postures while devil drums are beaten and trumpets blown. They whip the air with long rawhide whips and shout, daring the devil to do harm in that territory. These services end with the burning of the devil's image in a great bonfire outside the temple courtyards but just within the circle of sacred stones. Men, women, and children come from the surrounding encampments and take a lively part in this warning to the devil.

Lamas have many ways in which they read the future. The most common is the use of the breastbone of the sheep. The bone is cleaned and dried; then it is placed in a fire and burned well through. The fire produces different cracks and lines in the bone. From these lines the priest calculates an answer to whatever question he may have been asked — whether it is safe to start a journey, if a certain date is auspicious for a wedding, if a certain well will be a good place by which to pitch the yurta, and so on.

Lamas also use square bone dice. The dice are thrown three times into a silver bowl while the lama thinks of his god. The way the dice fall reveals to the priest the answer to any question.

Old brass coins lie buried in the soil of Mongolia.

They continually work to the surface, and while to the Western explorer they reveal facts concerning an early civilization, to the Mongol they are possessed of magic power. The priests use them in combinations of nine for divination. The nine coins must be of nine different kinds. The priest has one special coin which he believes to be of superior power to the others. This he places in his mouth and breathes heavily while he holds his lips closed. At the same time, with a circular movement of his right hand he spreads the other coins on the palm of his left so that they lie in a circle from east to west. From the position of the coins in his hand and the marks of his breath on the coin in his mouth he tells the inquirer where a lost horse is to be found, whether it will rain, if a sick relative will recover — anything one wishes to ask.

Very few lamas understand the prayers they repeat, as they are in the Tibetan language; but most lamas never hesitate to make use of a prayer. Many lamas are continually mumbling prayers and fingering their rosaries. I always wonder what they can be praying about. Once I inquired of a lama what he really could get by prayer. He told me that he could get anything he wanted. For instance, once he wished to go out and steal a horse, so he repeated thirty prayers from a sacred book; then he went out and he was very successful — he brought home a good horse.

There are many lamas who live quiet and decent lives, but there are others who are very wicked, and these constitute a large percentage of the thieves and criminals in the country. They are supposed to be tried and punished as other criminals are, but because of the superstitions surrounding them they get away with a lot of things that other folk could not do.

The son of one of my old teachers has done one wicked trick after another — but he has risen steadily, rank by rank, through Lamaism until he now holds a high office and is looked upon almost as a god because of the good luck he so often has. Once he desired to buy clothes, food, and other things from Kalgan. He went to the encampment of some people who were pious believers in Lamaism, and arranged for a man of the family to drive an ox and cart down to Kalgan for him. Just before they got to the city he picked up two stones from the dry river bottom and wrapped them in paper. They were about the same size as the lumps of silver then used as money. He put them in his leather traveling bag and locked them up. When he got to Kalgan he went to the principal Chinese merchant and asked for the head man. When the shop owner came he greeted him politely and then asked him if as a favor he would lock his money up safely. The merchant put the lama's bag into his big cash chest and locked it up.

The lama knew that word would be passed round the town that he had left his heavy money bag with the head merchant of the town, so he went from shop to shop and chose the things that he desired, and was handed goods on credit. He loaded all the things on to the cart and sent the man and ox he had borrowed back toward Mongolia. He himself stayed behind for two days. He spent them busily inquiring in many money shops the rate of exchange from silver to cash currency. Then, when the cart had had time to get far away on the plain, he slipped quietly out of town. The merchant waited two days for the lama to reappear; then, in conference with the other merchant creditors, he opened the bag and found only the two big stones.

Another time this same lama got four hundred sheep from a Chinese farmer in Chahar. He promised to pay at the end of two months. As soon as he had taken over the sheep he invited innumerable friends to come and feast with him for a week. He had several sheep killed every day, and there was a great merrymaking. Mongols to whom he owed old debts heard of this and pressed him for payment, so he paid them in sheep. Finally the Chinese merchant heard what was happening. He came and begged to have the sheep back. The lama finally allowed him to take all that were left of the sheep on condition that he would make no claim for the sixty or seventy that were missing by that time.

Another time he borrowed a fine horse and a saddle that was richly ornamented, and also a suit of lovely silk clothes. With these he accoutred himself as a very rich lama, traveled into a part of the country where he was not known, and bought thirty horses on credit. Herdsmen brought the horses home for him. He gave them to people to whom he owed money, or as presents to friends. The owner eventually came for his money. He heard how the horses had been disposed of and discovered that the lama had nothing. He was glad to make an agreement to take back the five horses that had not yet been given away.

Another time some rich Mongols desired to pasture their herd on a plain where there was plenty of grass but no water. He heard of this, and told them that he would show them where they could dig a well which would give them plenty of water if they would give him some cattle, sheep, and goats. As soon as he had received these animals he pointed without hesitation to a place just in front of him and said, "This is the place where you should dig." They dug, and they actually struck water. The lama told me afterwards that it was sheer luck.

He also carried medicine and read prayers, and had exceedingly good luck in curing the sick. So, as he has always had a keen interest in collecting all the material goods he could, he is now a very wealthy lama, with large herds of horses, cattle, and sheep.

In this way many lamas wander easily through life without worry.

But there are many good, honest men among the lamas. I have lama friends who are not only genial and nice as companions, but honorable, broad-minded, and intelligent. The Mantechirre Lama is one of these. He used sometimes to live in Urga, and it was there that I first met him.

Later he asked me to visit him in his monastery on the south side of the Bogda-Ol, about fifteen

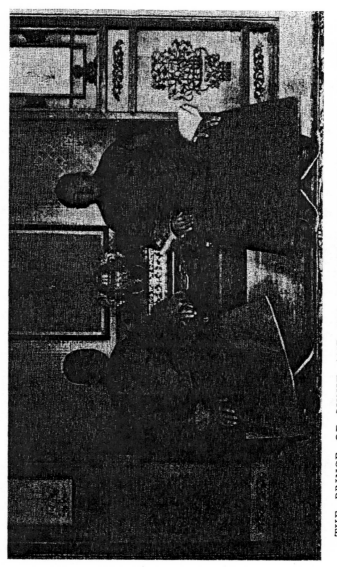

THE PRINCE OF SUNIT AND HIS BROTHER, THE HEAD LAMA OF THE
STATE LAMASSERY

miles from Urga, on the opposite side of the mountain. This is a very picturesque place in the forest-covered hills where reindeer graze within sight of the temple, and after my first visit I went there many times for a quiet rest when the things of the world seemed to press too heavily on me. Pilgrims from far and near constantly go there for his blessing. Nobles and high lamas are pleased to call him teacher. He is a quiet, gentle, scholarly man. He always asks me innumerable questions about the life in other parts of the world. He likes to hear how people live in Sweden, and what our religious men read and teach.

The Tsai-Di Lama is a man to whom I was introduced by the Living Buddha. Thirty years ago he was a minor lama, in charge of one of the Living Buddha's horse herds. Eventually he was promoted to mastership of the Buddha's racing horses. Later, during the Living Buddha's régime as Emperor, he served as Minister of Finance. He continued until his death in a very simple way of life, although quite wealthy. He owned many thousands of good horses. He always lived in a small but comfortable yurta. I have spent hour after hour with him, talking about this horse and that.

There was no famous race horse in the country during his lifetime of whose history he was ignorant. He used to reside near Urga in the winter, but in the summer he moved his yurta out to a hillside where the horses grazed. I bought from him many thousands of horses. His word was always dependable. We never had any written contracts.

Another friend was the Jalang-Se Lama, from the West of Tibet. He was very friendly to me from the first time I met him, and exceedingly anxious to learn everything he could about the civilization of outside countries. He was eager for Mongolia to adopt every modern idea that would improve the country. He had never seen a railway or steamboat, a motor car or a flying machine, until he made up his mind to go out of Mongolia and look at these wonders. He asked me to accompany him, and we had a most interesting tour. He was an ideal traveling companion, always courteous and generous.

When my friend, Roy Chapman Andrews, the American explorer, told me that he desired to work in North Mongolia, I went to the Jalang-Se Lama, who was then Prime Minister of Mongolia, and asked him for help. He met my request with intelligent energy. It was his influence that made the expedition possible.

I knew intimately a lama called Onchit. He was a doctor, and he always carried with him a supply of herb medicine. He helped many sick people, and as he was wealthy he never took payment from the poor. He lived in the encampment of his family, where I visited him many times. I had extensive business dealings with him and I always found his word dependable. He lived a virtuous life. He never drank or smoked. He would not reside in a temple, as he did not approve of temple life. He often said that many lamas were so bad that it was a shame that they should be priests. He had the best head for business of any Mongol that I have ever met, and he managed his herds in such a capable way that when he died he left his family exceedingly rich.

Women as well as men become lamas, but they do not live in the temples. It is a common thing in Mongolia for a woman, at the age of forty, to have her head shaved and go through the ceremony of entrance into lama priesthood. After this ceremony a woman is supposed not to live with a man any more, but to live a pious life in her home.

Although most women lamas are elderly, I know one woman who became a lama when she was only twenty-four. When I was traveling across country I sought shelter in her encampment from a storm. She housed me in a big guest yurta and supplied me with an abundance of food to eat and milk to drink. She had then about seven hundred horses, four hundred camels, many cattle, and thousands of sheep.

She manages her affairs with authority and dignity, keeping everything in perfect control and order. She is a tall, beautiful girl, and I asked her why she had become a lama at an age when she might have married and had a husband to look after and work for her, as well as been the mother of children. She answered that she lived a happy life and was sure a husband would only give her trouble and sorrow. She was very entertaining, and we played dominoes together while the storm raged outside. She has prospered during the years, and is an honest, capable, pious woman.

I have also known four incarnate priestesses. One

of these was a girl of twenty-two when I first met her. She was healthy, strong, and comely. At that time I was with the Foreign Bible Society, and had made camp not far from where she lived. She used to come to visit me almost every day, and talked about the Books of the Bible, some of which she took with her to read. She always rode up on a beautiful horse which was decorated with bright colors and silver ornaments. At the end of each of her visits, when we went to my yurta door, we always found a crowd of Mongols waiting outside to receive her blessing.

IV

THE LIVING BUDDHA

THE Living Buddha was born in Tibet. When he was a baby, lama priests took him to Urga, saying that it had been revealed to them that he was a holy child sent to be God on earth to the Mongolian people. The Mongols accepted him. His training was entirely Mongolian, yet through him the Tibetan priests had considerable influence in Mongolian affairs. His fun-loving personality captured the hearts of the fun-loving Mongols. They not only worshiped him as a divine god, but eventually they appointed him Emperor. His political position in Mongolia, even before his coronation as Emperor, was analogous to that of the Popes of mediæval Christendom.

My first meeting with the Living Buddha illustrates how easily a foreigner can be put into a foolish position by a little learning in the language of the country into which he has newly come. It was in 1894, when I first went to Urga. I was at that time working very hard at the study of the language, and had a good teacher. One day when I had finished my daily lessons, and felt very much in need of exercise after a cramped two hours of writing instruction, I ordered my riding horse and went out alone.

I had not gone very far when I saw a party of

lamas, dressed in flowing yellow robes and mounted
on frisky horses, coming at a good pace toward me
on the same road on which I was riding. I heard
someone shout "Bo," but as the only meaning I knew
for "bo" was "gun," and I did not have a gun, I
paid no attention. Suddenly I noticed that everyone
was staring at me, and shouting, "Bo! Bo! Bo!"
Still I did not understand, and thought it very strange
that all the people, save the lama party, had dismounted and were standing by their horses.

One of the lamas detached himself from the party
and galloped up to me. He stopped at my horse's
head and shouted right into my face, "Bo." I did
not understand, and, returning his stare gravely,
explained that I did not carry a gun. At that he, as
well as the crowd, burst into laughter. He pointed
to the ground and motioned to me to get off my horse.

I dismounted and stood meekly at the horse's
head. The lama turned his horse and dashed back
to his party. They all galloped up past me, smiling
and laughing in a manner which made me feel a
lunatic. As soon as they were out of sight I made
my shortest way home and presented myself to my
teacher.

I told him what had happened — how I had been
ordered to give up my gun when I did not have one
and forced to get down from my horse while the
party passed. He then explained that the word "bo"
has several meanings and that one of them is to get
down from a horse. From my description he knew
that the party of lamas must have been in attendance
on the Living Buddha, also out for his afternoon ride.

He told me that by the law of Mongolia every man, woman, and child must dismount when the Living Buddha passed.

This incident roused my curiosity about the man whom my teacher told me was worshiped by all the people of Mongolia as a god who even in the eyes of kings and princes could commit no sin. Consequently I often chose a road past his palace for my place of exercise.

One day, shortly after my first sight of him, I found a vast crowd of several thousand jostling, laughing people, packed into every possible nook and corner; but as I am taller and stronger than most men, I succeeded in pushing my way well in to the centre of the good-natured mob.

I supposed that I should witness some religious ceremony, so you can imagine my surprise when a window in the upper story of the palace was flung open and a jolly man, dressed in a gown of glittering gold, appeared and flung out a lady's corset. It flew over my head. I caught it. My impulse was to fling it back at him, but before I could do so someone snatched it out of my hand.

My very fair hair made me a target in that crowd of dark men and women. The man at the window noticed my discomfort and clapped his plump hands with delight. He hurled down a large bottle of perfume, which broke. The people sniffed the air and made faces at the odor.

A shower of watches followed — good watches of Swiss manufacture. There was a terrific scramble for these; men and women went mad, jumping on top of each other in their eagerness; but fortunately the Mongols are not only of most amiable disposition, but strong and sturdy, so no one was actually hurt. After the watches came clocks, all of foreign makes, and of many types. Most of them were delicate, dainty things, such as ladies admire; but he heaved out one tall grandfather clock, which fell with a thud and was broken to pieces.

Lamps followed the clocks; then more perfume. He disappeared from the window. The mob called him to come back. They cheered when he returned with his arms filled with Western ladies' dresses. These he threw out one at a time — evening gown of silver lace, riding habits, walking costumes of tweed, and a very much beruffled wrapper that fluttered down like a balloon.

Hats which must have been designed to match each costume were tossed out as if they were so many cakes. Both men and women put these on over their own headgear. The Living Buddha even tried one, — a concoction of straw and ostrich feathers, — and thrust his head through the window for the admiration of the crowd before he threw it down.

Shoes came next — high-heeled shoes of leather and of satin. These were followed by a shower of face powder punctuated with fluffy puffs. There were even a pair of skates, a toy windmill, a Noah's ark, and a small sailboat.

He ended the afternoon's sport by scattering hundreds of horns and whistles and some Christmas-tree tinsel. Then he closed the window. The Mon-

THE LIVING BUDDHA IN HIS SEVENTEENTH YEAR

gols cheered, blew their horns, and whistled through their fingers, calling him out again. He threw the window open and thrust out his empty hands; then the people dispersed. All that afternoon and evening they rollicked through the streets on horseback, blowing the whistles and the horns like children on circus day in Sweden.

Later, when I had come to know the Living Buddha as an intimate friend, I discovered that he had an insatiable curiosity concerning all Western things; and, since he could not go abroad, he received catalogues from shops in Stockholm, Berlin, London, Paris, Rome, and New York. It was his custom to order a sample of each article that interested him, so that he had frequent consignments of foreign goods arriving at his palace on the Tola River.

To make room for new things, and also reasoning that it was silly to keep material objects that had already served their purpose by informing him as to what foreigners use, he would proclaim a day on which he would distribute Western goods from the palace windows, and the jolly crowd I have pictured would collect at the appointed time. The performance gave a lot of pleasure to hundreds of fun-loving Mongols, and the Living Buddha enjoyed it immensely. I did too, on those occasions when I was asked to assist him.

When I had lived in Urga some time, had made many friends, and had become familiar with the language, a young Mongolian duke, the eldest son of the Prince of Hanta, invited me to go with him to the Dolan Horsone Natam, or the Festival of the Seven States. This was a festival held by the Living Buddha at a place some distance from Urga. People made preparations for it throughout a three-year interval by getting together the best possible outfit of clothes and by training the best race horses; and they looked forward to the absolution of their sins by the Living Buddha's personal blessing. It was by far the biggest show of splendor and of gayety held anywhere in Mongolia, and people flocked to it from all over the country.

The young Duke of Hanta had spoken to the Living Buddha about me and had asked for permission to bring me along, so I had the honor of being one of the Living Buddha's own party when he left Urga for the place of festivity. Consequently I went in company with the young nobles who escorted the Buddha when he went abroad on state occasions.

There were one hundred young laymen, all, except me, nobles in the Mongolian government military services; also an equal number of young lamas. We were all mounted on firm white horses. One hundred additional white horses unsaddled and unbridled were driven along by herdsmen with lassos who caught a fresh mount whenever one was needed. The laymen all wore long gowns of green, brown, or blue silk embroidered in bright colors in patterns according to their position, rank, or inherited right, and had round hats of Manchu style with the button of rank and the peacock feather. The lamas were in yellow robes of the most gorgeous brocade.

The Living Buddha rode in a beautiful cart covered

with gold silk and luxuriously cushioned. The wood-work of the cart was of the finest workmanship, polished until it shone like a mirror, and studded with gold nails. The two wheels were placed very far back so as to minimize the jolting of the cart. Shafts passed under the cart from the axles of the wheels and extended out in front of it, and a long pole was laid across these shafts.

The Living Buddha, very jovial, pulled his robes about him and got into the cart. When he was comfortably settled, he gave the order to start. Four young nobles then dashed up, two on either side of the shafts, lifted the pole, and placed it carefully in front of their saddles. Then we were off at break-neck speed.

When I had told a friend in Urga of my invitation to be one of the escort he had expressed doubt as to whether I should be able to keep up with the Living Buddha's party, who were all noted as very fast riders. I felt that the invitation was a challenge to Swedish horsemanship, and that I must prove that a young Swede could ride with the best young Mongol.

The Duke of Hanta had also been chaffed by his Mongol friends when he told them that I was to come along, and he desired very much to prove me a good fellow to his companions. He had made special provision for me by adding his own favorite white horse to the Buddha's herd for my particular benefit.

The white was a powerful animal and had no intention of being left behind the rest of the gay party. He was a beautiful animal to ride, intelligent and responsive, so that all I had to do was to sit in the saddle and enjoy his glorious movement as we swept forward well at the head of the party.

When we had gone about two miles, four other nobles exchanged places with the first four men who had carried the cart pole. The exchange was made so skillfully that the cart never stopped — only slowed a little. The herdsmen had ready four fresh horses. These they brought up for the four nobles who had been carrying the pole and whose horses were a bit blown with the exertion of dragging the cart. The riders dropped behind only an instant to change mounts. This change of duty took place frequently, as all of the nobles were eager to have an opportunity to serve the Living Buddha.

When we had gone little more than six miles, or about half the distance between Urga and the place of the festival, we crossed a very high hill. When we had passed over the summit the party halted by a clear spring where servants were waiting with refreshments. The Buddha came out of his cart and bade us all welcome to the repast which he had ordered to be spread here. We sat on the ground and had tea, cakes, and cheese.

After the repast we went forward again at the same rapid pace. As we came out of a valley, between hills covered with forest, I saw a small plain stretching out before us. This plain was covered with tents made of new white felt, and a few blue cloth tents, ornamented with sewn-on white patterns, were pitched among them. They made a very lovely sight, dotting the plain below the wooded mountains.

We conducted the Living Buddha to the largest and the most gorgeously fitted tent of all, and dismounted. He came out of his cart and thanked us for our escort and disappeared into his private tent.

The Duke of Hanta and I then remounted and rode to the cluster of tents that flew the banner of the Prince of Hanta. Here we were given a very cordial welcome by the entire family, and supplied with bowls of refreshing mare's milk.

This drink is called "arc" by the Mongols. It is not intoxicating, but very refreshing and strengthening. It satisfied both our hunger and our thirst. It is made by keeping the mare's milk in a rawhide bag so that evaporation takes place in the hide. It feels cool like ice water.

When we had been refreshed and had talked a little, the Prince of Hanta conducted me to a new white felt yurta pitched next to his own. This abode I shared with a young Mongol nobleman whom I had met earlier in Urga, called Prince Lob-Tsen Yen-Tsen. The tent was in the inner circle of the cluster of family tents, in the same position as the tent of a well-loved son.

Prince Lob-Tsen Yen-Tsen was a nobleman well known and liked by all the nobles of Mongolia. He was selected to share my tent and was asked to make me his special charge. He introduced me to people and answered all my questions concerning the things I did not understand.

The Duke of Hanta spent most of his time with us, although he had his own tent which he shared with another Mongolian friend.

There were about twenty thousand people gathered for the fair from all the states in Mongolia. I did not see anyone at any time who was not dressed in the best quality of silk, of the most brilliant colors. All my friends changed their costumes several times in a day, so I concluded that this was the general custom.

The women here, as in Western society, wore by far the most elaborate apparel; they were all in bright colors — never a pastel shade. But these bright hues suit the Mongolian type of beauty. They wore heavy gold and silver headdresses made in the shape of crowns. All these crowns were jeweled, and many women had clusters of pearls that hung down to their waists. Lob-Tsen Yen-Tsen explained to me that a woman's headdress might cost many thousands of dollars. He pointed out to me one beautiful young lady who had the equivalent of a herd of five thousand horses on her head.

Every woman wore coral, the national ornament of Mongolia, somewhere in her headdress. The women all wore riding boots similar in pattern to men's boots, ornamented with patterns of colored leather at the top.

At the festival everyone moved on a horse. No person seemed even to consider the possibility of walking the few yards from one tent to another; in fact, it would have been dangerous to do so, because no pedestrian was safe amid the galloping movement of the half-controlled horses. Hobbled horses stood before every tent, waiting the pleasure of the owners.

The horses, as is the Mongolian custom, were dressed almost as gayly as the men or women who rode them. Their bridles and their tail straps were all studded with silver and gold, or ornamented with gems, according to the fancy and wealth of a rider. The saddles were padded with scarlet placed over leather guards on felt pads, and were also ornamented with silver and gold.

Over the tents flew the bright banners of the different tribes, and on them were sewn royal colors, the inherited right of each noble family.

On the hillside and the grassy plain surrounding the tents were horses for racing, mares and cows for milking, and flocks of sheep to provide fresh meat for each day. They were tended by herdsmen and shepherds dressed in flowing garments of brilliant color, with streamer hats.

The festivities lasted for eight days, which were principally devoted to the horse races. The Living Buddha occupied the place of honor at each day's race. He was always gorgeously robed in gold and surrounded by a brilliant escort of priests and princes who sat about his outdoor throne.

The races were for different types of horses on different days. Any horse bred in Mongolia could be entered. The prizes were not large, — a roll of silk, or a little lump of silver, — but the honor of entering a winning horse was very great. The Mongol owners bred their stock with this thought in mind, and entered their best in each contest. To us Westerners there would seem perhaps to be a drawback in the fact that each winning horse must be presented to the Living Buddha. But the Living Buddha was so looked up to by all the Mongol people that every man and woman considered it an extremely great honor to have reared and trained a horse fit for his herds.

The winning owners were the heroes and the heroines of the festival. The Duke of Hanta continually pointed out to me men and women who had won in previous years, and spoke of them with admiration.

The races on the first day were for pacers, on the second day for two-year geldings, on the third day for three-year-olds, and on the fourth day for five-year-olds. On the fifth day all the races were between grown-up stallions. The sixth-day races were the most important and exciting of all. They were between geldings trained specially for racing. Entered in this event were horses from every state — the best that could be exhibited.

The jockeys in all the races were little boys or little girls between seven and fifteen years of age. They were all dressed in small silk jackets and very short silk pants. A few saddles were used, but, as the Duke of Hanta explained to me, jockeys had been badly hurt and even killed at former festivals when their saddles slipped and they were caught in them, so saddles were looked upon with disfavor by the owners, the crowd, and the jockeys. Consequently nearly all of the horses were ridden bareback.

The track was not specially prepared; the races were a test over the ordinary grass turf of Mongolia. The distance was ten miles. These long races were certainly an endurance trial for the horses, but an even more severe trial for the child riders. During every race some were thrown by their mounts. Their horses always ran over the rest of the course and came in loose. The children were picked up and looked after by outriders and starters who followed each race.

At the end of some of the races jockeys fell off their horses when they came to a standstill. They were picked up and carried away to be worked over. Several of the child riders could not speak, even to answer congratulations when they won, until they had rested for some time.

The Mongols are skillful in the treatment of riders who are stricken with temporary paralysis from overstrain, and they are soon revived. They are not permitted to sit or lie down, but are held up and walked slowly about until they are able to speak and to move alone. Despite the hardships of jockeying in races, I have never yet met a Mongol child, noble or commoner, who was not eager to ride. Especially was this so at the Living Buddha's festival.

The Mongolian people are inordinately proud of physical prowess and endurance under continued exposure to hardship. It is in the air their children breathe from birth!

The Duke of Hanta, who possessed herds numbering over ten thousand, had horses entered in nearly all of the races. He won first place in the pacers, snatching the prize from his father's horse, which was expected to win but came in second.

My friend, Lob-Tsen Yen-Tsen, won second place in the three-year-olds and first in the stallion race. He presented his winning stallion to the Living Buddha with a very good grace, although he confessed to me that he had expected to breed many future winners from him.

The Living Buddha had a great many of his own horses at the festival. The Prince of Hanta and I looked them over together, as we were much interested in the Living Buddha's horse, which had won the gelding race for the last three seasons. He was a beautiful animal, a big bay with four white socks and a white star in his forehead, and appeared in very good condition. But we knew his age, and the Prince of Hanta said that two or three other horses would press him very hard for first place this time.

We went on to the inspection of a horse that a prince from the east was entering for the same race. It was a younger animal, of cream color, with long slim legs and well-developed running muscles. I was very much attracted to this horse from the instant I saw him, and gave little attention to the other animals in the three or four additional herds that we visited.

The hour of the race came. The horses got off in fine order. With the Duke of Hanta I rode to the rise of a hill from which we could watch the first part of the race, and then around to another hill from which we obtained a view of the open valley in which the last stage was run. It was very easy to follow the progress of the cream horse because of his light color. In the same way the white socks of the Living Buddha's bay marked him on the course.

These two entered the valley running neck to neck.

The cream, my favorite, gained slowly inch by inch until the bay's nose was only level with his tail. There was only a little way to go — I thought that the race was the cream's without a doubt, and relaxed the strain with which I had been leaning forward in my saddle. But something happened. I cannot be certain that the jockey pulled his horse to the left — the little boy must certainly have been too exhausted to do that after ten miles of galloping bareback on a strong horse. Still, the bay came in winner, filling out the circle of his fourth season.

At the end of each day's race the Living Buddha went back to his tent; then rows on rows of people knelt about the tent on the green grass, their bowed heads low on their hands. Prostrate and humble, these rich noblemen from all over Mongolia awaited the blessing of the little Tibetan boy, now grown to manhood, who the lama priests had told them was sent to earth to reveal to them the will of God. He would come out of his tent and walk among them, touching each one gently on the head. Then they would rise and go back to their own tents.

When the hour of blessing was past they shook off their seriousness and were a gay people seemingly interested in nothing beyond horses and frivolity. And the Buddha too, when he had done his duty, would be one with them in merriment.

Mounted on horses, all the people dashed about from tent to tent, visiting and feasting with their friends, the women as free and gay as the men. They made tests of horsemanship over the same place where the races were run, dared each other to ride this horse and that, and sang songs and played flutes until all hours of the night.

During the first six days of the fair wrestlers from all over Mongolia met in preliminary contests in Urga. The winners in these wrestling matches came down to the Dolan Horsone Natam and pitted their skill against the Living Buddha's own wrestlers on the seventh and eighth days of the fair. Any citizen of Mongolia who wished to do so, whether he was a lama or a layman, could enter these wrestling contests.

Both Lob-Tsen Yen-Tsen and the Duke of Hanta thought it would be a great joke if they could induce me to enter. They teased me and dared me, but I knew that any contestant who succeeded in worsting, in a match, one of the Living Buddha's wrestlers immediately became the Living Buddha's property, and, as I told them, I am a free-born Swede.

A Mongol considered it a very good thing to win a place as one of the Living Buddha's wrestlers, because he was housed, clothed, and fed for the rest of his life by the bounty of the Buddha, and was a respected and honored citizen of Urga. All the Living Buddha's wrestlers were dressed in lovely silks. He was very proud of them, and treated them with extreme generosity.

On the seventh and eighth days of this festival five men won wrestling matches. The festivities of the eighth evening lasted through the night. I dined in the Prince of Hanta's own tent. From there we visited the tents of a dozen other princes, and talked with men from all parts of Mongolia. I got a very comprehensive idea of the whole country through these introductions to the rulers of the small states of which Mongolia is made up.

On the morning of the ninth day the Living Buddha returned to Urga, escorted in the same manner and at the same speed as when he came. I again rode the Duke of Hanta's white horse for the first half of the journey, and in the second half I had an equally spirited and intelligent white horse from the Buddha's herd.

From the day on which I was first introduced to the Living Buddha he was always exceedingly kind to me and most solicitous for my comfort.

One summer, when it was unusually hot in Urga, he invited me to stay with him in his palace on the Tola River. I hesitated to accept, as I thought that the invitation was just an act of politeness; but he continued to send for me to come, so eventually I went for two weeks. While I was there every possible thing was done for my pleasure and amusement. The Living Buddha saw to it that I had an interesting time; and his wife, who managed her large household with marvelous smoothness, looked after my material needs.

The Buddhist religion forbade the Living God to marry, but when he fell in love with a vivacious, handsome Mongolian girl, the Mongolian people found a way. There was a most elaborate ceremony. She was created a goddess. After she had become a goddess there was no reason at all why she was not a fit mate for a living god.

In fact, by all reason, a god was the only person that a goddess could marry. The Mongols never spoke of her as a human being, but always as a goddess. She was a practical, sensible woman, and a splendid home-maker who drove from the Buddha's great palace any gloom that may have lurked in its many corridors before she came. She was a jolly companion, a good horsewoman, an excellent shot. The Buddha was exceedingly proud of her.

During the two weeks that I was at the palace she and I went every morning to the Sacred Mountain for target practice. One day the Living Buddha said, "Now we must have a contest so that I can discover which of you is really the best shot."

He ordered a target to be put up, then handed each of us a rifle. He especially stressed the fact that the one he gave me had come from France and was very expensive. His wife fired three shots and made as many hits in the mark. I then took careful aim, but registered three misses, to the Buddha's huge delight.

After examining my gun I noticed that the sight had been knocked to one side. I called the Buddha's attention to this. He laughed loud and long, and said, "If you are really a good shot, you should have noticed the condition of your gun before you aimed."

He was always fond of a practical joke. Some years after this, when I took him the first motor car that was ever seen in Urga, — a Ford, — he connected the electric current with the body of the car, and then invited the highest lamas and nobles to come to tea. After tea he exhibited the car, and he asked his guests to feel the fine polish on the fenders.

The first man to touch the car drew back as though burned. The others laughed at his timidity. Then a second one put out a brave hand — and jerked it back. More laughter, led by the Buddha. He took the greatest pleasure in this tea party at which his friends received such a shock that not one of them would consent to ride with him in his car — they all marveled at his own ability to sit in it and ride comfortably through the palace grounds.

The Buddha had a feast every year, when all the best wrestlers from all over Mongolia met to try their skill and strength in wrestling matches. These were gorgeous, colorful affairs which the Buddha attended in rich dress, surrounded by a brilliant escort.

Sometimes the Living Buddha asked me to sit in the place of honor next to him to watch the wrestling. At one of these wrestling festivities a giant Mongol took part. This Mongol, from the western provinces, was nearly eight feet tall, broad, and strongly made. He came into the wrestling ring stripped, wearing only a silken girdle and a pair of high riding boots.

The Living Buddha, who was always ready for fun, ordered a small lama, the smallest in Urga, into the ring to meet the giant. This lama was noted for his quickness and catlike grace. The expectation and excitement of the seven thousand onlookers were intense. They pressed close against the barrier of the outdoor ring. The two men sparred with each other without coming to grips, shifting and moving, each

hoping to get an advantageous grip on the other,
the agile little wrestler scarcely reaching as high as
the waist of his opponent. At last the tiny lama ran
between the legs of the giant. He clasped him just
above the knees, and gave a mighty jerk. The giant
fell with a heavy thud. The audience roared with
laughter. The poor giant rose, very red in the face,
and went away, scratching his head. He never
showed himself in Urga again.

The Buddha lived in a luxurious way and surrounded himself with every object that his fancy
desired, fed on the richest and the most costly foods,
drank expensive French champagne, and dressed
himself and all his attendants in the most gorgeous
apparel. But he was a very kind man. No poor
person, priest or layman, ever came to him in trouble,
during all the years that I knew him, and went away
without the Buddha having done everything in his
power to make the suffering one's lot more easy. His
charity extended into the far corners of the country
that knew him as the Living God. He also had infinite compassion for all creatures of the animal
world.

To the south of Urga, near his palace, there is a
fine mountain called Bogda-Ol. During the Living
Buddha's life in Mongolia all hunting and killing of
animals was forbidden on this mountain. Here one
could see, any day of the year, big herds of reindeer,
wild bears, wolves, foxes, mountain deer, and hundreds of kinds of birds, all quite tame and not at all
afraid of man.

A MONGOLIAN FROM THE WESTERN PROVINCES
NEARLY EIGHT FEET TALL

The Buddha constantly collected his animals from
other places and had them freed in this paradise —
apes, bears, rare birds, and even an elephant. Likewise in the River Tola, which runs by Urga, the
Buddha forbade all catching of fish.

In 1911, the people of Mongolia sent the Manchu
governor back to China and decided that their
country would be better governed without further
coöperation with China. A delegation of kings,
princes, dukes, and commoners went to the Living
Buddha and asked him to become emperor. He con-
sented. The inauguration of the new emperor was
a very impressive ceremony. The whole of North
Mongolia flocked to Urga in festive robes. The
streets were paraded by Mongolian soldiers mounted
on beautiful horses and dressed in rich uniforms.

The people presented to the Living Buddha, as a
thank offering for his consenting to be made emperor,
three hundred white horses with yellow halters, each
with a red fox skin tied about its throat, and one
hundred white camels, each with a sable skin tied
about its throat. These were led up to the palace
and presented to him. Then the nobles, kings,
princes, and commoners all promised allegiance to
the new emperor, after he had taken a solemn oath.

The Emperor soon selected ministers and officials.
His government ran smoothly. The best blood of
Mongolia flocked around him. This was a prosperous
time for Urga. Life was very gay, and hope ran high.
It was a good season and wealth abounded. Chinese
and Russian merchants did a fine business. Trade

throve throughout the empire during his régime. There were no heavy taxes. The roads were filled with big caravans going and coming constantly, winding down across the plain through Kalgan to China, or northward into Russia. Mongolia prospered as she has never prospered at any other time during the years that I have lived among her people.

The end of the régime was brought about because of the generosity and the goodness of the Mongols' character — a too great trust in all men, a simplicity which judges others to be as honest as they themselves are.

In November 1919, a Chinese general, Little Hsu, under pretense of protecting the border, obtained permission to bring an army through Urga. However, on getting his army to Urga he broke the Kiakhta Treaty and made himself master of North Mongolia. He was a shrewd and sharp little man and did his work quickly. Nobles who entertained him were thrown into prison. He seized Urga in a cruel grip.

Two different parties of Mongols set out trustfully to Russia to get help against this army. One party went to Moscow and invited the Soviet authorities to come and help. The other party went to see Baron Ungern-Sternberg in the mountains to the east of Urga. The Mongols did not realize that Russia was then a divided country. In their eyes its inhabitants were simply the Russian people, a signatory party to the treaty that had been broken — genial and just traders with Mongolia for more than a century. The Mongols knew nothing of "Red" and "White." If they had heard the words, they did not comprehend them.

Baron Ungern-Sternberg was nearer, and reached Urga before any authority in Moscow could act. He attacked and took Urga in February 1920 with his army of seven hundred and fifty Russians and as many more Mongols, destroying most of Little Hsu's army of fifteen thousand men. He was now ruler over Urga and North Mongolia. But although he was a cruel soldier of fortune, he had great respect for the Living Buddha and treated him and the Mongol nobles fairly. The Living Buddha was treated as Emperor, but in reality had little power.

Baron Sternberg was an energetic man. He opened a big tannery in Urga, installed electric light, and built and repaired many bridges. But he was obsessed by a hatred of all Jews, and put to death with terrible cruelty all the Russian Jews in Urga that he could lay his hands on, — men, women, and children, — despite everything that the Living Buddha and the Mongolian people could do. His régime was of short duration, for the Red Russians came in from the north and defeated and killed him.

The Russian Red Army entered Urga in July 1921. They gave the Mongols assurance of their independence, and promised assistance in the fulfillment of the Kiakhta Treaty. But as their political views were against emperors and princes, the Living Buddha never regained his former splendor or power, and all nobles soon disappeared from North Mongolia. Commoners, advised by Russians from Moscow, were the power in the new government. The

Living Buddha sickened and died in 1924, and it seems that there will never be another Living Buddha in Mongolia.

He was always very kind to me. He made me many valuable presents, and decorated me with the Mongolian ducal decoration. He was a sick man when I took my friend, Sven Hedin, to visit him. He was nearly blind, and his heart had been broken by the turn of affairs in Mongolia. But he did everything in his power to make Hedin's visit to Urga a success.

He was not only the Living God who gave absolution for their sins twice weekly to Mongolian supplicants at Urga, but a great man who recognized genius in other men when he met it.

V

MARRIAGE AND OTHER CEREMONIES

WHEN a Mongolian boy or girl reaches the age of seven years it is customary for the parents to begin to look about among their friends for a suitable engagement for marriage. The lamas of the near-by lamassery are always consulted in this matter, and the horoscope of both children whose parents are considering a preliminary engagement is at once taken by a priest.

If the comparison of the horoscopes shows that the children were born under stars favorable to a prosperous and peaceful union, then the parents of the girl invite relatives and friends to a feast. This is called "the feast of the small white scarf" or the "first engagement."

The parents of the boy bring their young son with them to the festivities and the little boy kneels before his little fiancée and holds his two hands, palms upward, in front of him. On his upturned palms there lies a white silk scarf, and on the scarf two silver earrings, the gift and the symbol of the first engagement. The girl's ears have already been pierced as a small child, in readiness for this gift. She takes the earrings from his hands and puts them on. This is the pledge that if they grow up suited to each other they will follow this first ceremony with a formal engagement when they are about fifteen.

If all has gone well with both families and their children have grown up healthy and wish to follow the engagement with marriage, the parents of the girl again make a feast. This is a much more serious and elaborate affair than the first. Only the girl's relatives attend it. The family are busy for many days before, preparing for it. The relatives assemble, dressed in their best clothes, and feast.

The parents of the boy are not invited, but they send a special delegate, who presents a big silk scarf and a pair of bracelets to the daughter of the house in whose honor the feast is held. If she accepts them, this is a pledge that she will accept the betrothed in marriage later.

By the offering and the acceptance of this large scarf and engagement bracelets the honor of the boy and the girl and of both families has been pledged. This ceremony must be followed by consummation in marriage within three or four years. The girl is never supposed to know the exact date for the marriage until the day arrives, or to be present at home when preparations are made for it. It is customary for her to go to visit the woman highest in rank in her family during the preparation for the wedding festivities.

I have attended more weddings in Mongolia than I can count. My first Mongolian invitation was to the wedding of the son of the ruler of the state of Ordos. Since then I have been present at the weddings of commoners and of nobles. I find the ceremony practically the same throughout Mongolia, north, south, east, and west, differing only in nonessentials

— that is, it is simple or magnificent, in accordance with the wealth of the parents of the bride and groom.

Not long ago I attended the wedding of the daughter of a wealthy commoner who was married to the son of the ruler of a state where I often visit. When I arrived at the encampment of the family the girl was away visiting her aunt. The encampment buzzed with activity. Twenty new white cone-shaped tents made of wool felt from the spring clipping had been pitched about the family tents, ready for the reception of guests. They were gayly furnished with bright carpet cushions and low redwood tables. In each yurta there was a heap of soft furs piled up on a low framework ready for guests to make themselves comfortable beds. In addition to the white felt yurtas, there were seven new blue cloth tents ready to shelter servants and herdsmen and to provide additional space for banquet preparations.

Butchers had slaughtered oxen and sheep; cooks had roasted, boiled, and seasoned them by every recipe they knew; bakers had secured flour from Chinese dealers and made bread, cakes, and golden crullers; cow's milk had become great mounds of butter and white mountains of cheese. The women of the family had distilled wine from mare's milk. Chests of fine garments had been opened, and needles sped through new cloth, making raiment ready for the adornment of the family. Men, women, and children ran hither and yon on innumerable errands, busy from dawn until the light of day failed.

Above the noise of all this bustle rang the hammer of a goldsmith as he fashioned a magnificent headdress for the bride. Her father, anxious in his pride that his child should be adorned as befitted the bride of the heir of the reigning prince, spent hour after hour hovering about the smith, admiring or criticizing, and changing his design. Again and again he slipped away to his treasure chest and returned with yet another treasured pearl or piece of old coral.

When he showed me the finished headdress I saw that pearls would lie on her fair brow, seven strands of pearls would fall on either side of her young face and drop until they touched her knees, and fourteen loops of equally lovely pearls would hang down her back until they touched the hem of her gown. Priceless jade would adorn her shoulders. Smooth old coral fastened in hammered gold swung in many pendants, and rubies gleamed in the mesh cap ready for her glossy hair.

Relatives had been invited from far and near to come to the marriage festivities. Some had already arrived when I got there; the others rode in and were welcomed soon after.

Dressed in bright silk, the girl's relatives and immediate family made the encampment a brilliant moving mass of color. The marine blue, sapphire, olive green, purple, lavender, wisteria, and rose gowns of laymen and women, heavily embroidered with butterflies, flowers, and birds, mingled with the crimson and yellow brocades worn by the lamas.

The girl's brother was sent to his relative's encampment to bring her home. The aunt and her family came back with them. When the group reached the top of the hill which overlooked the encampment of the girl's parents, she saw the preparations that had been made in her absence, was startled, and, turning her horse round, made off across the plains. But her brother soon caught up with her, grabbed the bridle, and pulled the horse back toward home. She then leaped from the saddle, but her cousins caught her. Matrons of the family, who had waited behind a clump of shrubs just below the hill, ran forward and closed about her in a tight circle. The most recently married woman among them flung a thick blue veil over the maid's head. Thus blinded by the swathes of the veil, she was carried through the encampment and put down on the felt-padded floor of her own tent. Then her relatives withdrew, leaving only the aunt with her. The door was fastened securely on the outside.

Throughout the day and most of the night the gorgeous assembly gathered for the wedding feast made merry. A band of musicians strolled about playing gay music. They lingered now in the great banquet tent where the father entertained the men highest in rank among the guests, or passed into the glittering throng of matrons gathered in the tent of the girl's mother. They made their way through the entire encampment, penetrating to where the herdsmen and servants gathered round steaming bowls and full tankards, omitting only the one tent where the girl lay in darkness.

In places where shadows might have dimmed the gayety, tallow dips sputtered, throwing out pools of yellow light from many-branched holders. Stars twinkled in the sky. The moon shed a silver radiance on shining dresses and sparkling jewels as the romping merrymakers roamed from tent to tent.

Only in the tent of the girl there was darkness. At dawn the servants took tea in to her. A little while later her girl friends and younger sisters forced their way into the tent. They sat in a circle about her and sewed the girdle of her dress fast to their own — a symbol that they thus held her in maidenhood with them.

A large party of mounted nobles rode in from the west. Clouds of dust heralded their arrival. A hundred strong, mounted on fine horses, they were a magnificent sight, clad in the most brilliant raiment the imagination of a color-loving people could conceive and the wealth of princes execute. They led a riderless white horse that arched his neck and lifted his feet high, shaking his golden bridle and rattling golden stirrups against white doeskin saddle guards.

At the hitching place the girl's family welcomed the party from the palace. The ceremony of greeting and method of procedure were so elaborate that more than an hour of formal phrases was necessary before the last "You go first" and "No, you; I am not worthy" had been exchanged and all were seated in the great reception tent in the exact order of precedence and the exact place that he or she knew was his or hers by inherited right.

All the visitors were greeted and honored, save the young bridegroom-elect — a slender boy of seventeen. No notice was taken of him. Ignored in silence, he was permitted to enter last and wait unobtrusively in the lowest place by the yurta door.

The representatives of the two families were seated on cushions in two rows facing each other, the highest in rank of the two households in the left and right places nearest the altar. The first of the visitors cleared his throat significantly. There was perfect silence. In sonorous tones he repeated the speech wherein have been poeticized the formal words with which a Mongol daughter shall be asked for in marriage.

When he had finished, a servant knelt and presented him with a silver cup of wine on a white scarf. The wine and the scarf were accepted. Then the man of first rank in the girl's family quoted the formal response in rolling phrases. Again the servant knelt and offered wine in a silver cup on a white scarf.

When the second speaker's parched throat had been relieved, another man among the visitors took up the cue. After him came another answer from the drama prepared through the ages past. So on and on, with wine ceremoniously offered to each speaker and as ceremoniously accepted. Sometimes the orators were women, sometimes men.

The vocal play came to an end, and servants entered with garments carried on extended arms: underclothing of soft silk; boots of finely tanned leather, ornamented with elaborate stitch patterns; a long rich satin gown embroidered in golden thread; a beautiful sleeveless jacket — all made for the bridegroom in the home of the girl. An attendant pulled off the shy lad's usual apparel and dressed him in this new outfit. Now he was invited by the girl's family to come and sit on a cushion.

While food and drink were pressed upon the con-
fused and flushed boy, deputies were dispatched for
the bride. A struggle ensued in her tent, where the
girls fought to hold her against her elders. Some of
these girls were flung into corners, others were pushed
roughly inside the door, as their friend was carried
away. One, stronger than her companions, clung on
even outside, until the grip of her fingers had to be
loosened by a sharp blow.

The maid, still wrapped in the mist of the blue
veil that had been flung over her the previous afternoon, was put down on the ground outside the reception tent. Here she lay, in her plain dress, soiled and
wrinkled now — the dress she had worn the day she
traveled home. She reminded me of a crushed blos-
som in the centre of that gorgeous throng.

Women lifted her to her feet, and the man highest
in rank in her family knelt beside her and begged her
to accept a silver bowl of milk with a lump of butter
floating on the surface. Her mother raised her veil
and pleaded with her to drink, reminding her that
the pure white milk was symbolic of their pure love
for her, while the golden butter was the token of
that love's genuineness.

The daughter humbly bent her lips to the silver
brim and took a few sips. Then a red silk cape was
quickly flung over her dress, and a large red hat was
dropped over her blue-veiled head. Her jeweled
headdress was not adjusted over her hair, but fastened
round her neck so that it held the veil down even
more closely than before.

The white horse was now led up. Strong arms

lifted the inert girl into the golden saddle. The spirited horse snorted and reared. Men brought the nervous animal down again. Sharp voices commanded the girl to give aid and take charge of the wonderful mount the prince had so kindly provided for her use. Her relatives strove to rouse her pride as a horsewoman, but she gave no answer, and would have been thrown had firm hands slackened their control.

Men with hands on each side of the bridle led the horse a few paces, while relatives on either side of the girl kept her in the saddle. All the rest of us had now mounted — all the girl's relatives, men and women, young boys and girls, as well as all the palace party. Our horses were restless to be off. The girl was lifted down from the saddle and put into a cart, into which had been thrown soft furs, covered with a spread of red silk. A horse was fastened to this two-wheeled cart. The aunt got in with the girl. A mounted herdsman took the leading rein, and we were all off at breakneck speed over the trackless plateau, the cart that contained the bride-elect careering madly in our midst.

At the first neighbor's encampment women rushed out. They dashed furiously in among our horses and jerked the lead rein from the herdsman's hands. They soon had the cart stopped and gathered about the maid with words of comfort. Other women followed them out of the yurtas with tea and cakes with which they begged the girl to refresh herself. She thanked them, and made as though to leap from the cart, but her aunt struck the horse and he bounded ahead at a frightened gallop. After another hour we sighted the tiled roofs of the palace in jagged outline against the sky.

The girl was taken from the cart and put on the white horse again. Riders kept close around her, holding her in the saddle and guiding her mount. When we came to the palace we all dismounted on the green slope below the Eastern Gates, where tents had been made ready for the festivities.

A small altar spread over with a cloth of satin had been placed on the grass. The bridegroom and his personal attendant knelt before this altar. The bride was led to stand near them. An official offered her a silver basin of milk in which floated butter — a token that this new household welcomed her with pure hearts and would be true to her. The girl was then taken away by the women of the palace, to rest in a private tent. All the rest of us were conducted to the places that had been arranged for our comfort. All was quiet until flute players summoned us to come for a feast.

The best viands that the state could supply were served on low tables around which we sat on brilliant cushions. Dish after dish followed in lavish abundance. As the servants brought food, the ruler of the state and his wife, the bridegroom and his brothers and their young sister, went from group to group, serving each guest, on bended knee, with a silver cup of wine. Lastly, filling the cups already six times filled, came the bride, still blinded by the blue veil and guided by the bridegroom's elder sister, who also served wine.

Above the clatter of crockery, the scurrying of servants, and the hum of conversation, music swelled from throats and from stringed instruments strummed with the fingers or played with a bow like a violin.

As time advanced, the wedding party grew more and more merry. Guests joined with minstrels in the singing of ballads recounting the historic romances of famous Mongolian lovers.

At sunset the lad and the maid were ceremoniously conducted to a big white felt yurta which had been prepared as a bridal chamber, and were left there with the girl's aunt.

In the festival tents and on the sloping plain the music continued to throb with sentimental melody. At midnight a second feast was spread. Again the ruler and his wife, with their three younger sons and their two daughters, offered silver cups of wine to each guest on humbly bended knees, murmuring wishes for peace.

After this we all retired. Next morning tea and cakes were served in our tents, so that all who desired to do so might rest until late. For the entertainment of the more energetic, wrestling matches were staged between the prince's soldiers and the young lamas from the state temples. Flutes announced the first feast of the day sometime past noon.

Then the bride came out from the palace and walked among the people who had gathered to pay her homage. She wore golden slippers and a long gown of lavender silk with a short white satin jacket embroidered in gold. Her head was crowned with her glossy hair arranged in smooth coils and weighted by the headdress which was both her dowry and the symbol of her matron's estate. She conducted herself with magnificent regal dignity — gracious, yet unapproachable. All of us who looked at her talked of her amazing beauty and her queenly manner.

That afternoon there was horse racing, followed by another banquet. The next day a final feast was served in mid-morning, as it is the custom in Mongolia for wedding guests to take their departure before noon on the third day of celebration.

Guests most distantly connected with the bride took leave of her first, going to bid her farewell in the bridal chamber, where she sat ready to receive them, dressed in a gown of jade green, over which her lovely pearls fell like drops of morning dew. She accepted all the congratulations with cool dignity, until at last her own family came to kiss her good-bye.

I had known her since she was a tiny child, and her father insisted that I wait to bid her farewell with her own immediate family. As we came to her, her haughty poise dropped from her like a player's mask. In a broken voice, with tears streaming down her cheeks, she pleaded to be allowed to return to the encampment of her father, but her parents turned deaf ears to her entreaties. When she rose from her seat to follow them, they pushed her back on her royal cushion and put heavy stones on her silk skirts, to symbolize that she was fastened to the place where they had set her. They reminded her that by the common law of Mongolia every girl must fulfill the engagement she makes in company with her parents when she is fifteen years of age, and that after the wedding ceremony she must live three days and three nights with the man she has married.

The other side of this law — written so deeply in the hearts of the freedom-loving Mongolian people that even an absolute monarch dare not override it — is that when the youth and the maid have risen to manly and womanly wisdom by three days' and three nights' experience either may end the marriage at will without explanation other than the desire to do so. After that each may live· alone or marry again without any further divorce or any second marriage ceremony.

On the morning of the fourth day I rode back to the palace with the girl's father, in company with his eldest son and his eldest brother, both lamas from the state temple. We were accompanied by an escort of mounted men who carried three cooked sheep and three big baskets of bread. The girl's brother led a saddled riderless horse. We were received in the bridal chamber. The bride was seated on the same cushion on which she had sat when we took leave of her.

Her father knelt before her and told her that her family now offered her the opportunity to return to them. His attendants brought her three silver platters on each of which lay a whole cooked sheep and three platters heaped high with cheese. He said, "This is token, my daughter, that your father is both willing and able to provide for you."

With a gesture the daughter bade her father rise

to his feet and ordered the palace servants to remove the food. This was an indication that she was satisfied with her marriage and did not now wish to return home.

Marriage has no religious significance in Mongolia; it is a civil contract. Its binding force is the mere will of the man and the woman, and either the man or the woman is at liberty to end it. When the marriage is dissolved soon after the wedding there has to be an adjustment of wedding expenses. If the bridegroom is the one who desires separation, he must repay the bride's parents for the cost of their part in the wedding; if the bride is the dissatisfied party, she must refund the groom's parents what they have spent.

In Mongolia women have equal rights with men in the regulation of affairs, with the exception that in divorce the children of a marriage remain with the father unless one or all of them is of sufficient age to decide which parent is preferred.

When a man and woman have lived together some years and have come to disagree, they separate without consideration of the wedding expenses. Each takes his or her own personal property, and they divide yurtas and herds in proportion to what belonged to each at the beginning of their union.

There is no moral censure of divorce. The Mongols reason that when a man and a woman cannot live together harmoniously they are better apart. Each can now pitch his or her tents in company with relatives, or alone.

The Mongol woman is quite as capable of managing

MONGOLIAN WOMEN

the affairs of life as the man. From childhood the girl is accustomed to long intervals of time in which the men of her family are absent from the encampment, leaving the women to look after themselves. She knows how to tend the flocks and to do all the necessary things. Even in young girlhood she makes long journeys on horseback alone, seeking shelter in encampments throughout the country she crosses as independently as a boy. If she chooses to live alone, she knows how to take care of herself.

There are no restrictions concerning the remarriage of either party in a divorce. Only the first marriage is celebrated with ceremony, such as I have described. In later unions the couple usually give a feast to friends and relatives at which they announce their marriage, but this is not really necessary. Often couples simply join tents and herds without even the ceremony of a celebration feast.

In summer, during the fifth or sixth month, the exact date being a matter of personal choice, each family in Mongolia offers sacrifice to the God of Earth. This is done on the top of the highest hill overlooking the place where the family are encamped.

In Mongolia all high hills have what is called an "obe" on them. An obe is a compact pile of stones, every stone placed by a sincere believer in worship of the God of Earth. In the heart of this heap of stones is buried a sealed casket containing Tibetan prayers, saints' charms, and other precious things. Should a family happen to pitch their tents below a small hill where there is no obe, their first act is to call lamas from the nearest temple and make one.

Sometimes precious jewels and treasures that the family believe have given them good luck are put in with the prayers in the casket. A tall pole stands in the middle of the heap of stones, and silk banners, with prayers written on them, are hung on it.

It is the habit of Mongols when traveling through the country to place one more stone on each obe they pass. They are specially careful to observe this custom when returning from a journey. Each stone placed is then a thank offering to the God of Earth for a safe arrival at home again.

The worship of the obe is a combination of the old Mongolian nature worship, which dates back into prehistoric times, and Lamaism, which came from Tibet by the conversion of the wife of Kublai Khan.

The worship of the God of Earth is performed by one family alone or by several friendly families joining together. The prince of every state also makes sacrifice in the summer of every year in the name of the state.

Worship of the God of Earth begins on a very dark morning, an hour before sunrise. People make their way up the hill as best they can in the darkness. Lamas cluster on the left side of the obe, and lay folk on the right. The priests beat drums made of the skull bones of a young boy and a maid, to drive away evil influences. Then the lay people prostrate themselves on their side of the obe and call upon the god to listen. The priests chant prayers, following which the lay folk again prostrate themselves and plead with the god for mercy.

A glowing fire of dried dung is built. While it grows red and hot, the priests chant prayers, beat their drums, and blow trumpets. The headman of each family approaches the fire, calling out to the god that he has come in the name of his household to offer sacrifice. He puts the whole body of a previously cooked sheep into the fire and draws it back again while the flames lick round the tallow, throwing a rosy light on the obe. After the mutton offering, this same headman (or all the headmen, if there are several families) offers cheese, milk, butter — something of all the things received as a gift from the earth.

At this time, and at other times, if the wolves have been bad, or if the grazing is not good, horses, camels, cattle, sheep, and goats are dedicated to the God of Earth. When animals are to be offered they are ranged in a circle round the fire. The horses have the first place, and the other animals come in the order of their importance.

Only young and perfect animals are dedicated to the god. The prince or commoner who makes the offering selects the best foals, baby camels, calves, lambs, and kids born since spring. Priests say prayers over each animal in turn. The laymen prostrate themselves before the obe and cry out to the god in prayers of adoration for giving them animals. They declare that this season's number has been greater than they have deserved, and beg the gracious God of Earth to take back a part of his gift.

The head priest then fastens in the mane or about

the neck of each animal a ribbon of four colors —
green, blue, red, and yellow. The assembled crowd
break into a prayer of exultation. When dawn comes,
the colts, calves, camels, lambs, and kids so dedicated
are loosed and turned into the herds and flocks.
Thereafter they are spoken of as the God of Earth's
animals. They can never be killed, sold, or used by
man, but remain on earth until the god calls them
away. They must be cared for even more lovingly
than those animals man calls his own.

In every herd in Mongolia there are these animals
that cannot be put to domestic use. Even the poorest
family has at least one sheep in its care which belongs to the God of Earth. Wealthy people have as
many as a hundred of their best horses which they
regard as belonging to the god.

This is the custom all over Mongolia. One of my
progressive friends listened one year to my advice
against this custom and did not dedicate animals to
a life of uselessness at the time of the midsummer
festival, but later, when I stopped at his encampment, I found he had made the sacrifice. He explained: "I had to do it. The God of Earth was so
angry because I did not that he let the wolves take
terrific toll of all my flocks and herds. Since I have
made my prayers and given back a part of my riches,
as experience has taught us Mongols we should do,
I have not lost one animal. All have thrived un-
molested; we have had rain and good grass."

The Mongol people make a festival of every possible occasion. After the seriousness of the early
morning obe service they always have a holiday.

That is why several families or a whole district prefer to worship together. Then there are more people to join in the gayety afterwards. Men, women, and children dress in their best clothes for the festival services, so they are all ready for their holiday. When they come down from the hill they have a big feast for which the women have prepared an abundance of food during the preceding week.

It is the custom to set up new festival tents of blue or white — often gayly ornamented with bright designs — in the valley below the hill for the day of merrymaking. After the morning feast the time until noon is spent in wrestling.

Lamas are just as keen for fun as lay people. A throne is always built overlooking the wrestling place, for the incarnate lama of the near-by temple. On either side of him are thrones a little lower, for the senior priests. The young men, lamas and lay-men, take part in the wrestling matches. Anyone in the family or families who has made the sacrifice, or any passing Mongol who wishes to do so, can enter for these wrestling contests. Musical horns are blown and people chant songs as each wrestler dances into the ring.

Often there are half a dozen bouts going on at the same time. When one contestant is thrown by another man, he is considered beaten. Then the winner dances and makes a low bow to the priests and the headman of the community or family. He is given a prize — a little piece of dry cheese. He claps his heels and his hands together, makes another deep bow, and dances back across the wrestling place, throwing the cheese north, south, east, and west to the God of Earth as he passes back into the crowd. He can wrestle again if anyone whom he has not already beaten challenges him.

The afternoon is always occupied with horse races. Sometimes two or three horses from the same herd compete. An owner often tries horses from his different herds against each other. The races, like those I have described, are of ten to fifteen miles, and are run in a circular course, so that they begin and end at the same place. Here also the prizes are little bits of cheese, which are thrown to the God of Earth.

The day often closes with music. It is considered a fine thing for a person in the family or a visitor to play the violin or the flute and to lead the singing of old folk tales.

On the last night of the twelfth moon the Mongols worship Heaven. To the Mongol the God of Earth ranks above the God of Heaven. It is the God of Earth who furnishes all man's material needs, so he is the more easily understood. There is gratitude in the heart of every man, woman, and child for horses to ride, food to eat, clothes to wear, and a felt tent to keep out the cold. The God of Heaven is an abstract, far-away deity to the practical-minded people of the plateau.

Yet that same quality which made Kublai Khan offer homage to all the great saints of the world equally still persists in his descendants, who do not neglect Heaven entirely. So, on the last day of the year, they make a feast in their yurtas, and after the feast they go out and build up great pillars of snow. They have a merry time doing this, frolicking as they roll big snowballs down to the place which they have chosen for the pillar and pile them one above the other. When they have worked at making it high until they are tired, they stick twigs and branches all over it. Tied to each of these twigs is sheep wool which has been dipped in melted unsalted butter.

Then all the people bow down round the snow pillar and call out to the God of Heaven, chanting prayers of adoration. The headman of the family takes flint from his flint pouch and strikes fire to a bit of butter-soaked wool. Using this as a torch, he lights all the butter-soaked banners. The family join with him. Sometimes a snow pillar has a thousand banners.

I have ridden through Mongolia on a New Year's Eve night when the whole plateau was lit up by these pillars of fire.

The Mongols make sacrifice to the God of Fire at the time of the winter equinox. Fire has never ceased to be a thing of wonder and magic to the people of the plateau. Centuries of time have not made commonplace for them the fact that out of a bit of flint can come a force which makes light and heat. Every Mongol man, woman, and child possesses a flint case. The home of fire must be fittingly housed, so even a person who must dress himself in rags provides at least a silver case in which to carry his flint. Wealthy people have jeweled cases.

No Mongol would thrust his feet toward a fire,

spit into it, or show lack of reverence for it in any way. Fire is a god.

The Mongolian winter is severely cold. The Fire God flashing out of a tiny bit of flint makes the heap of dried dung which is the Mongol's fuel, and a contemptible thing, to live and glow, warming the tent and making it light even after the sun has gone down.

When the cruel winter has set in, the sun in the heavens does less for the Mongol than at any other time of the year. But the Fire God does not desert him; he heals and comforts him after a long ride across the plain, gives him hot drink and appetizing food. The Mongol worships him with reverence, sacrificing to him some of the best of everything that he possesses.

The day of the big fire sacrifice the yurtas are cleaned and made gay, the fire brazier is polished with mutton tallow until it shines, and fuel is heaped up lavishly. All of the family dress in their best clothes. The men put on their ceremonial coats embroidered in bright colors, polish their silver ornaments with sand, and grease and shine their boots. The children have new clothes, if possible, and wear earrings, bracelets, and finger rings set with coral, which is the color of fire. The women adorn their hair with their complete headdress, of silver or gold, set with jewels.

The most important part of the sheep, the breast, has been cooked until the meat has fallen off. The white bone is filled with butter, cheese, tea, and a choice piece of meat cut out from near a sheep's heart. The sheep bone, filled with these titbits, is wrapped in a rich silk scarf by the mother of the family. The father brings fire with his flint. The daughters take silk streamers and dip them in melted butter. These streamers are blue, yellow, green, red, and white. The lama members of the family chant prayers.

The children lay a flat latticework of dry birch twigs over the glowing fire. The father puts the offering, wrapped in a silk scarf, on this lattice, and each of the women throw on a scarf of one of the five colors. Then every other member of the family throws some offering into the fire.

As the God of Fire roars his appreciation of these gifts all the family bow down and worship, giving praises to the god and asking him to keep all evil out of their lives and send only good. The part of the sheep which was not put on the fire is laid on the family altar, or, if the encampment has a "gods' tent," it is put on the shrine there. It must not be eaten for three days, but if the family wish to keep good fortune with them they must feast on it three days after the sacrifice.

This meat must not be given to strangers. To do so is to throw away the favor of the Fire God, as he will bring no good to anyone who is not present at the sacrifice.

VI

HORSES

THERE are no banks in Mongolia; horses are the currency of the country. For instance, if I ask a man what an article is worth, — a handsome snuff bottle, a jeweled headdress, an amber-stemmed pipe, or a coral-studded flint case, — he answers "one horse" or "five horses" or "five hundred horses" according to the preciousness of the thing. When a Mongol, as sometimes happens in trade with Russians or Chinese or other foreigners, does receive money he immediately invests it in his horse herd by purchasing as many animals as it will buy.

Under the surface of Mongolia lie rich deposits of gold and silver. For centuries the Mongols have known that the metal is there: it is pretty, and they have always taken what they desired for personal adornment or the adornment of their bridles and saddles. But they value it so lightly that it has never occurred to them to use it as currency. The horse has remained from the earliest recorded time the measure of wealth. The horse is placed first in their scale of material and æsthetic importance.

The horse is both for utility and for pleasure. Horse races are the most important feature of every gathering. Constant association with horses has not dulled the Mongols' pleasure in the beauty of a galloping herd racing across the green plain with floating manes and tails. Men, women, and children draw rein to watch colts frolic. A splendidly built horse is a poem to a Mongol.

Old folk tell with bright eyes tales of the strength, speed, endurance, and intelligence of horses they have known. From generation to generation the stories of famous horses are passed down; they are the folklore of a people who have no literature. Mongol children are lulled to sleep with the legend of Bosafabo, a red chestnut stallion with a white star on his face who lived in Donran cave in ancient times. Commoners, nobles, and even the Great Khan brought mares to him in the hope that he would sire their foals.

Bosafabo was intelligent, whimsical, fleet, and all-powerful. He was too wise to be controlled or bribed by men. Sometimes he drove the mare of a prince away and looked with favor on the mare of a commoner. He fathered a famous line of progenitors — horses brave and clever. Any wonderful horse to-day is spoken of as descended from Bosafabo.

The Mongols hold the horse in too high regard to use him lightly. They do not eat horseflesh. They do not put heavy burdens on a horse. The camel, the ox, and even the milch cow in necessity, draw their heavy carts and carry their packs. The horse is not tied up in a stall or confined in any way when not in use for riding; he roams free over the rolling prairie.

The Mongols are kind and loving with their animals — especially with their horses, who consequently have no fear of human beings. It was the horse that made it possible for the Mongols, in the time of Genghis Khan, to conquer half the known world. Until the age of mechanical vehicles the Mongol, who is from babyhood at home in the saddle, possessed the power to move most easily and quickly over the surface of the earth.

Mongolia is a rolling, undulating land, unbroken by the plough, uncut by fences or roads or railways, without towns or villages. It is an ideal country for motoring, and a land where there is no need to build roads — a motor car can be run in any direction over the turf. But while the Mongol is charmed by the aeroplane flying across the sky like a bird, he who has cherished the horse for centuries does not favor the motor car.

I usually travel through Mongolia in the saddle. But last summer I had occasion to go to an eastern state quickly, so I went out from my Kalgan home in my seven-passenger Dodge. I soon came into territory where the people had never seen a motor car; but they were not impressed by my horseless carriage. I stopped at an encampment to ask the way. The family who directed me told me that my long shining car was an ugly thing compared to the natural grace of a horse. They said it smelled bad, and warned me against using it lest I should get nose trouble from breathing air polluted by it. They wondered at my possessing it, as it was neither beautiful nor sensible, but supposed that Chinese bandits had stolen all my horses, so that I had none to ride when I left Kalgan.

One woman warned me that if I rode around on a

THE HORSE IS MONGOLIA'S GOLD

soft-cushioned seat I should get fat and unhealthy. When the winter came I should be in poor shape, and might die. She advised me to abandon the car and borrow a good horse, and even offered to lend me one; but I must not leave the foul-smelling car near her tent.

Through the centuries stallions and mares have come into Mongolia from the far corners of the earth. Early records tell of a vast camel-caravan trade with the Middle East which tapped the horse-breeding areas of Turkestan. Chinese historians comment on a system of barter with the peoples of Persia and Arabia by which they received horses that were in turn bartered with the Mongols of the plateau, "who value the horse first among all things," for furs, wool, cattle, and sheep.

The armies of Genghis Khan scoured the country from the Yellow Sea to the Levant, penetrating even to Moscow, selecting the best horses for military purposes from the country they passed through. They chose horses with the idea of increasing the speed, the weight-carrying ability, and the power of endurance upon meagre sustenance of their own breed.

Genghis established his empire over half the world. One Chinese writer noted numerous gifts of horses: "One thousand white-nosed mares as a gift from Crepé Noyon"; "Juchi, Genghis's first-born son, brought his father a present of one hundred thousand huge bay horses from Russia." Another memorandum tells of a gift of stallions bred in Poland. In the accounts it is recorded that Genghis and his son and his grandson drew tribute in horses from all the territory under their rule.

Marco Polo, who visited Kublai Khan in the thirteenth century, was amazed at the vast herds of horses that he saw at ceremonies, on the hunting field, and in use as horse expresses by which the post was carried at miraculous speed through the empire. He was struck with the endurance, the speed, and the intelligence of the Mongol horses.

So, according to history, in time of peace and in time of war the Mongol people have been drawing foreign stallions and mares into their herds to interbreed. In the Chinese wars of 1860 the punitive forces from India had many stallions in their cavalry. Mongolian princes who saw these animals coveted them; they secured all they could and took them to the plateau.

Again, in 1900, when German, French, Italian, and British forces were sent to North China to rescue their nationals from the antiforeign fanatics, nicknamed "Boxers," they all had with them in their cavalry mares and stallions. Of these a goodly number found their way up into Mongolia; they were either bought by Chinese dealers and bartered on the plateau or given as gifts by those in authority to Mongol princes. Notable among the gifts were fifty mares and five stallions presented to the Mongol prince Hara Ching by Sir Purtab Singh. These were horses bred in India.

A few years later, at the end of the Russo-Japanese War, the Mongols secured many Russian stallions. Some of these were wounded, others were very war-weary, but they soon recovered health and strength on the Mongolian plateau.

In addition to what the Mongols have done alone, in very recent years there have been some experiments attempted by foreigners. In North Mongolia the Russians have brought in Siberian stallions, hoping to increase the size of the horses on the plains. The Catholic missionaries in the Dolonor district have also imported stallions with this same idea in mind — to increase the size. German farmers in the east are also making the experiment.

I have felt that I could improve upon the Mongol's method by selective breeding, and since 1904 have brought into my herds various foreign stallions. My experience is that the first colts from the English and Australian stallions are leggy and lacking in hardiness. The Arabs are a trifle more successful. Most of the colts sired by these foreign stallions do not survive the first winter. The third generation are short, stocky, and sturdy — not radically different from the other colts of my herds.

Climatic conditions tend to thin out of the herd in the Mongolian plain all except the horse possessed of unusual endurance. Only the strong characteristics of the imported strain persist; all characteristics that tend to weaken the physical strength of a horse are washed out by the fourth generation. The horse on the Mongolian plain lives by his wits; horses who have depended through generations on the intelligence of man are unable to cope adequately with wolves, blizzards, and the situation in which a horse must seek his own food. Stable feeding and watering of a breed weakens individual initiative in their descendants.

I think that the Arab is the most successful in combination with the Mongol horse, but a pure Arab — the offspring of an Arab mare and an Arab stallion — is not a success in Mongolia. Imported horses do not survive many seasons in Mongolia — excepting the Siberian horse, which comes from even a rougher climate.

If one examines any Mongol horse closely it is possible to find in it marks of the many different strains that have gone to make up its character. The muzzle particularly is indicative of the Persian, and the hoof of the Turkestan. The Persian strain persists, I think, because the Persian is bred where he too has often to go for a long time without food. The English thoroughbred does not perpetuate his quality on the Mongolian plain because the kind of life the European horse has lived for generations does not prepare his offspring for the hardships of the plateau.

The climatic conditions and the amount of water and food in different localities make a great difference in the horses in the various states of Mongolia.

In the Chahar district, that part of Mongolia which borders on China, the horses are, with a few exceptions, small, weak, and inferior. This is not because of climatic conditions. The winter here is less severe than in other parts of Mongolia; the grass is usually good from May until November; the snowfall is not terrifically heavy — the horses are able to get down to the grass every month of the year;

and in this district one can almost always find water by digging a well twenty or thirty feet deep. And indeed, although the appearance of the herds is bad, I have bought from here some notable horses that have made good records on the Chinese race courses.

But for nearly three centuries this was the imperial pasture land of the Manchus — while they were rulers of China. In this section Mongols were appointed to care for the imperial horses. By imperial order every imperial herd consisted of three hundred and sixty horses. The Manchus required that each Mongol who accepted a position as keeper of an imperial herd should supply them on demand with anything up to the number of three hundred and sixty animals.

In their account books the Manchus separated the keepers into the breeders of white, piebald, bay, chestnut, black, white-nosed, and star-faced horses. When they desired horses they sent up for a certain number, all of one color. Indeed, color was their sole concern; they cared nothing about grace of movement, beauty of carriage, endurance, speed, or intelligence.

The Mongols felt that since the Manchus lacked understanding of the good points of a horse it was folly ever to send a superior animal down to China. The herds bred every year produced a certain number of colts. These were sorted out, the best ones going farther inland to the Mongols' own private herds, and the poor ones being kept to make up the imperial three hundred and sixty. If it happened that a man

got an order to send down one hundred white horses
and he did not have one hundred white scrubs, he
traded round among his friends, sometimes getting
two animals for one, until he had a lot which he considered inferior enough to send to the imperial
rulers.

This continual picking out of the poor colts and
the breeding down through three hundred years to
what the Mongol considered was a good enough
animal for folk who did not cherish the horse as he
did has had the natural effect on the horses of the
Chahar district.

The middle of Mongolia, comprising that stretch
which is known as the Gobi Desert, has for the
greater part of the year such a scarcity of food that
only those animals that are very hardy survive here.
The horses in this part of the country attain their
full growth very slowly. The usual animal in this
district measures under thirteen hands, but I have
taken out of this area horses of six or seven years
and fed them well and found that in a year or two
they grew a couple of inches in height.

The sand in the grass which these animals have to
eat wears down their teeth, so that a foreigner looking into the mouth of one of them to discover the
age is certain to put it two or three years in advance
of what it really is. I have found that their teeth
also grow better if the animals are taken out of this
district and put into a good place, even after they
have reached an age when an ordinary horse would
have done with tooth growth.

When I look at the barrenness of this area I sometimes marvel that any animal can possibly manage to live here. The cold is not so severe as farther north, and there is seldom much snow to cover up what grass grows, but the rainfall is light and the soil looks like a sandy beach in many places. When rain does fall the desert grows green while one watches it.

The horses from this district are extremely game little animals. They make excellent mounts if one has to go on a long, hard trip. Their weight-carrying ability, speed, and endurance are astonishing in comparison with their size. This area has given the China race courses more than one surprise in past years; and the horses drawn from here were very useful to the Mongols in their last war with China, when by swift riding they trapped their invading foes.

Eastern Mongolia — that is, the part of Mongolia east of the Gobi — is famous as the breeding place for pacing horses. The Mongols like fancy pacing animals to ride. They are much sought after by women, lamas, and folk who want to make a good appearance, at festivals, weddings, and similar gatherings. Wealthy Mongols pay enormous prices for pacers.

Part of this territory is covered by deep sand, through which only sparse, coarse grass can grow, but other parts have rich velvet green turf, and are well supplied with water. This district is noted for the speed of the horses bred there, and, although a small state, has an excellent record as a place from which good race horses come. Its prince, and all his commoners as well, are very keen on producing the best possible animals, and are proud of every success won in competition against horses from other states.

Northeastern Mongolia, through which runs the Kerulen River, is the section of Mongolia most favorable to the horse. The whole Kerulen Valley has excellent grass, which means that the animals here have plenty of food and water from birth. They grow larger and stronger than the horses in any other part of the country.

Sanpeitzu, Talopetzu, and Tsetserban are the three principal states in this district. In addition there are several small states. "Sanpeitzu" is the magic name to Westerners and Chinese interested in racing. Horses from Sanpeitzu are not distinguishable from horses from the other states of Kerulen Valley, but the name has been popularized. Mongol dealers take advantage of this and call any horse from Northeast Mongolia which measures thirteen or fourteen hands a Sanpeitzu horse when they offer it for sale to the Chinese or the foreigner. Wealthy Mongols and Russians in this area are constantly importing outside stallions for the purpose of increasing the speed of the Kerulen Valley horse. Since the Russian advisers have come into power in North Mongolia, no mares or stallions are allowed to be exported from this area, and a tax of about one hundred dollars is charged on every gelding exported.

Throughout the whole of Mongolia the people are intensely interested in racing, and as their mode of life does not fill their days with toil they have a great deal of time for collecting and training horses for competition. As the Kerulen Valley is favorable to the horse, and North Mongolia was the home of the Living Buddha, around whom the wealthy nobles congregated, it was naturally in times past the racing centre of the country.

The Mongol's idea in a race is to test speed and endurance over a longer course than the Westerners ride. The shortest Mongolian race I ever saw was three English miles; the usual races are from ten to fifteen miles. The Mongol does not believe in a prepared race course. Mongolian races are run across country, under conditions identical with those which the horse will encounter if it is necessary for him to travel such a distance in an emergency.

In long races like these it is not always the horse of largest build that wins; in fact, more often than not it is the small, sturdy animal that comes galloping in first. News travels fast in Mongolia, and any horse that makes a record in a race is immediately sought after by many Mongols from different parts of the country. The owner and breeder of a winning animal is looked upon with admiration.

Many animals from the Kerulen Valley have made good on the short race courses of China, where small horses normally have very little chance against long-limbed runners. The demand from Chinese dealers for horses from this district has always been greater than the supply.

The horses in Northwest Mongolia, the Djasachto Han district, are small and undeveloped. The snows here come early and stay on until late spring. This gives a very short grazing season, and horses here are insufficiently nourished all their lives, the average size being under twelve hands. Those that do survive are hard, sturdy mounts for travelers.

The Altai Eli district has much better climatic conditions. There is good grass there and the horses are of a bigger type. Despite their size, these animals are, on the average, less speedy than a horse bred in any other district in Mongolia.

In former days the Manchu emperor used to order six or seven hundred horses from this district every year, asking always for pacers. They are fine-looking animals, and made a good show in a parade. They had to start a whole year before they were wanted in Peking so as to arrive there in fair condition. The route they took was through Uliassutai and across the Gobi Desert to Kalgan.

Southwest Mongolia, which encompasses the state of Ordos, is very sandy. The horses here are small in size and undeveloped in appearance.

Every horse in Mongolia is branded with the brand of its owner; but there is no universal regulation concerning brands, so that it is impossible to tell by the brand the district from which a horse comes. The ruler of a state has his own brand and each of his commoners has a distinct brand, so that within the state they can all keep their herds distinct no matter how often they borrow mounts from each other's herds when riding across country. Beyond this there is no attempt at distinction.

Any state can repeat the brands of another state. The most common brands used are the swastica, the half-moon, the three-ball, the triangle, and the two-bar. Some owners put their brand on the top of the hind quarter, others on the rear low down on the hind quarter, others on the shoulder.

All over Mongolia Mongols treat their horses in the same manner. They are run always in herds numbering from two to five hundred — of sufficient size to fight off the wolves that are an ever-present menace. The Mongols do not stable their horses; they run almost as free as a wild herd. No grain is raised in Mongolia and horses are never grain-fed; they subsist on grass entirely, foraging for their own food. When one rides a Mongol horse it must be turned out to graze at night to keep it fit. In winter they will dig down under the snow for their food. If the winter is long and hard, all the weak members of a herd die before the spring. Under these conditions the Mongol horse is bred for endurance and can go for a long period of time without food; on the other hand, his stomach is not upset by heavy feeding in those times when there is an abundance to eat.

The Mongols do not believe in forced mating. They consider it an outrage against nature for a herd owner to select animals and breed them together. The young stallion begins to collect his mares at the age of five years, and as only a few mares mate before that age his family is made up of wives of nearly the same age as himself. He makes his selection from the colts in the herds, generally to the number of fifteen to twenty. These he will keep together as his own band regardless of the size of the actual herd;

so that a horse herd is made up of a large number of smaller herds. These bands scatter for grazing, but come together immediately on the approach of danger, when they are commanded and regulated by the old stallions. There is usually one sagacious old fellow who takes charge in time of trouble. In country where there is no open water they all bunch together twice daily to go down to the well, where they are watered by the herdsmen.

Even in a stampede a stallion does not forget his family; if any of his mares or foals fall behind in the mad rush, the stallion circles around behind and shepherds them into the herd. Or he will trot at the rear to guard against wolves. A Mongol stallion's solicitude for one of his mares at foaling time is great. He clears a circle round her and walks about keeping any of the other horses from coming near. When the colt is born he fondles it affectionately, seems to have intense pride in its attempts to stand on its wobbly legs, and will defend it with his life an instant after birth.

During the season when the young stallions are collecting their mares there are continual fights between these youngsters. Sometimes these quarrels over a particular young mare colt last for days, during which the herd is kept in a turmoil by snapping, kicking young animals. A young stallion seldom attempts to steal a mare from the family of an older one; but in case he does, the older horse, clever in the ways of waging war, soon sends him about his business.

Some mares seem to be born coquettes and make

constant trouble in their herds. They appear to cajole stallions into stealing them, and then when the fight is on run back to their own group.

Mares in Mongolia are milked, since mare's milk is one of the principal foods. All young colts are broken to the halter during the milking season. Thus the colts are early used to man, and are generally easy to break to the saddle when the time comes. All colts are saddled in their second year, but are not ridden hard. It is the habit of the Mongol herdsmen to cut the tails of colts that have been broken, leaving one long strand that marks them as two-year-olds.

There are always more male colts born than it would be wise to keep, as they would kill each other in fights over the growing mares. The male colt that is not to be kept for breeding is castrated in his third year. The geldings in a herd usually stick together in bands of fifteen or twenty, but some geldings attach themselves to a stallion and his family.

The manes and tails of horses on the plateau grow very luxuriantly. Those of mares and geldings are sheared, and the coarse hair is used for making rope. The Mongols believe that it hurts the pride of a stallion to cut his tail or mane, so they allow them to grow naturally; often the tail drags on the ground, while the mane hangs to the front knees and bright eyes peer out through a thick, shaggy forelock.

The herdsmen always break some of each year's colts in as lasso horses. Each herd has a goodly number of horses that have been taught this work. The quickest and most intelligent are chosen for it.

The herdsman is too busy manipulating his lasso to be able to guide his horse as well. A lasso animal will put up a fight against being caught and will resist the halter, but once caught he stands still to be saddled and enters into the sport of lassoing others of the herd with zest.

When a horse is being lassoed there is great excitement in the herd until the horses understand which is wanted; then they take no more interest. If the herdsman misjudges his balance in the saddle, or throws his lasso so that the horse entangled can pull hard against it, he is often dragged off his horse. I have seen cases where a man has been dragged several times around and through a herd still clinging on valiantly until the second herdsman came to the rescue and threw another rawhide over the fractious animal.

The Mongol horse seldom lies down to sleep at night. He is on guard against wolves until daylight, when he takes what sleep he needs. Young colts often lie down to rest among the herd, but they are never stepped on, even in the rush to the watering trough. Very young foals scamper back and forth between the legs of the grown horses, romping like kittens as they try their growing strength, and even the worst-tempered grown animal does not kick at them.

As soon as there is any sign of the horses' common enemy, the wolf, the whole herd rush together, the colts on the inside, the mares in a ring around them with their hind legs out so that they can kick if attacked, and the stallions and the geldings ranging free on the outside. In the clear Mongolian air I

THE MONGOL LASSO IN USE

have heard the snapping of teeth a mile away when a fight was on.

The stallions and the geldings do not hesitate to attack a wolf, and give chase instantly one draws near, but wise old stallions do not let themselves be lured away from the mares and foals. A favorite wolf trick is for one or even more of their pack to attract the attention of a herd and try to get the strong animals to gallop after them. This leaves the weak unprotected, and other wolves leap in and make a kill. Then later all join in a nice feast. Herds with old stallions lose fewest of their young to the wolves.

Wolf hunts frequently meet in Mongolia. A hunt usually covers three successive days. The meet assembles in front of the state residence of the monarch or at the encampment of a wealthy commoner. As for every festival in Mongolia folk come dressed in their brightest colors, so for this occasion everyone is mounted on a strong, fast, sure-footed, intelligent horse.

The meet gathers soon after sunrise. Each person comes armed with a lasso. Before the party sets out, the host who has called the meet usually serves wine distilled from mare's milk. Each person takes his own silver basin out from the front of his garment and holds it to be filled from the host's great spirit jug. The party is quite merry and reckless before the hunt begins.

When the wine has been passed and all the folk expected have come, the meet sets out for the territory where the hunt is to be held. As they come near the place which has been decided upon as the scene of the first day's activities, the hunters spread out in a wide circle. Each person rides up on to a rock ledge or a hilltop, and two or three hunters gallop through the centre of the circle, shouting lustily to drive out the wolves.

A wolf, when chased, always makes for the nearest high hill. On the day of the hunt he usually finds a mounted man with a lasso on every hilltop. As soon as he sees the man the wolf turns and runs another way. So the hunt is on. Riders tear after the wolf, the horses entering into the sport with a fervor as great as that of their riders, for the wolf is the enemy of the horse in Mongolia from the instant of the birth of each.

Horses snort and neigh with anger, men shout at the top of their voices, the wolf scurries here and there striving with mad cunning to escape. The Mongols vie with each other to be the first to get a lasso over the wolf. These hunts are hunts without dogs. They are a test of the skill of man and horse pitted against the wolf.

The Mongol horse goes at full speed over rocks and ravines, down valleys, up hills, and over plains. When the wolf is tired out or cornered on some rocky ledge, he turns snarling to meet his foe. Then the Mongol must throw his lasso so that he can twist the rawhide thong in a way that will throttle the wolf to death, else the desperate animal will spring upon horse and rider.

The first man to kill a wolf is the hero of the day. The skin of each wolf killed is pegged out on the ground near the evening camp fire. The hunters sit round the camp fire talking while the food is made ready, then roll up in blankets and sleep until dawn, when they are up for the second day's sport. Fresh horses are used each day. A locality hunted through in this way is fairly free from wolves when the hunt is over. If a few do lurk in the rocky ledges, they are too frightened to attack the herds for some time to come.

The foaling season is the anxious time in Mongolia. It is then that the wolves takes heaviest toll of the herd. Sometimes in a herd where two or three hundred colts are dropped there will be only twenty or thirty left at the end of the year. Owners regret their folly if they have made too many gelding race horses and not left sufficient stallions to defend the young.

Foals dropped early after the winter snow clears do the best. They get the full benefit of the spring grass in the richness of their mothers' milk. They have both spring and summer warmth on their backs. They learn to forage for their own food while grass is still plentiful. Summer is the only time of year when horses in Mongolia have plenty to eat. As colts only feed well for a few months in the year of their birth and at intervals thereafter, they do not attain their full growth or mature as early as horses in the West who eat equally well the calendar round.

Every winter the colts that have not had a good long summer begin to die from lack of food and inability to resist the cold. A foal that begins life early in spring has a good thick coat ready for the blizzards when they come.

The Mongol horse thrives despite hardship, and does not seem to be disturbed by disease. Most herds tested by the Maline test are found to have some horses with glanders; but the Mongols laugh at the Maline test which foreign veterinary doctors consider so important. Any Mongol will take into his herd without fear a horse which the foreigner says has glanders. The Mongols say that the Maline test proves nothing; and in the open air on the prairie glanders never seems really to develop. A horse which is said by veterinaries to have glanders can be used for years in Mongolia without any further development of the disease.

The Mongol owner is most afraid of scab. There is a little scab in some districts, but even that does not kill many horses. The Mongols are very skillful at curing scab.

The Mongol horse is never shod, and although most parts of Mongolia are sandy, and other parts have sharp stones, the horse in Mongolia does not suffer from lameness. The hoofs when left natural grow very hard. I have ridden horses from morn until night, day after day, from herds in almost every state in Mongolia, and have never been troubled by their going lame. If a horse does hurt his foot in any way so that it gets tender, he is turned free in the nearest herd and is quickly well again.

Horses taken away from Mongolia, shod, and kept tied up in stables suffer from lameness very much. Shoeing seems to make the hoof grow unnaturally high, and the shoe places the horse's weight on muscles other than those he has been accustomed to use.

New Year's Day is the great holiday of Mongolia and the day of a unique horse race which has no beginning and no end, yet on which the reputations of horse breeders are made or lost.

On New Year's morning all the people in Mongolia dress in the brightest colors and the best clothes they possess. Even the poorest, tiniest child will have some gay ribbon tucked into his attire. People rise before the sun and hasten to salute each other with the usual snuff-bottle salutation, followed by the presentation of a silk scarf on outstretched hands to every friend and relative in the encampment. Then, after some tea and mutton, the real fun of the day begins.

Mongol encampments are scattered here and there over the country. There is such distance between them that it takes a day's hard riding for a Mongol man or woman to pay the calls to relatives and friends which are required by custom. The fastest and strongest horses are saved up for this occasion, and gayly dressed people gallop in every direction over the prairie.

This is a very special occasion for the herdsmen, because on this day, according to common law, the freedom of the herds is his. No owner can make objection if one or more of his very best animals are killed on that day. For months previously the herdsmen have boasted to rivals that they will show them the dust in this race.

The racers do not meet at any particular place. Each person starts out from his or her own home. Horses are raced until set of sun or until rider and beast are tired out. The gallop is from tent to tent, and the rule is that every rider must stop at every yurta he comes to long enough to give the New Year greetings, wish the occupants of the tent prosperity in their herds and flocks, and accept food and drink, which is prepared and ready in abundance on this day. Then, when a decent visit has been paid, the rider is free to mount again and tear away as fast as he can to the next yurta.

Mare's milk is brewed into wine for this day's celebration. Drinking bowls are filled with it in every yurta where the riders stop; consequently, as the day grows older, the Mongols become more and more lively. And the riding becomes more furious. Riders turn away from nothing. They go over stones, up hills and down, and across ravines. Sometimes there are nasty falls. But this is all in the game; nobody worries over such trifles. At yurtas where I have stayed I have seen Mongols arrive so drunk that they could not get down from the saddle alone, and they had to be helped to mount again. Once in the saddle, the Mongol, drunk or sober, goes at a mad pace.

On New Year's Day riders often sway to a dangerous degree from side to side of the horse, but because they are accustomed to the saddle from babyhood they manage to keep their seat. There are cases sometimes, however, where people get separated from their party, have a nasty fall in some ravine, and go to sleep deep in the snow never to wake up again. Such accidents are not very frequent, for the horses are sure-footed.

The horses seem to enter into the sport with even more zest than their riders, turning in to the hitching place at every yurta they sight, and galloping away again as soon as the rider's foot is in the stirrup.

The horse that stands up best under this strain is proclaimed throughout the countryside as a very good horse. It gives both the owner and the herdsman pride and satisfaction. A herdsman riding a black horse from one of my herds was credited with first place in the New Year race in his state last year. Immediately I had many offers for this horse. Even in far-away states I was congratulated by commoners and nobles, who had heard of my horse's prowess in the surprising way that news travels in Mongolia.

The horse on the Mongolian plain is possessed of surprising speed. The Mongols ride their horses at a gallop and cover distances in quick time. They know how to take care of their horses, though, and it is very seldom that one of them comes to harm. As soon as a horse shows fatigue, he is allowed to go free in the herd, where he can set his own pace and yet have the constant exercise that hardens his muscles.

I have a friend in China who is keenly interested in racing horses in one of the port cities. He came up to Mongolia one time, and was so amazed at the speed of the Mongol horse that he set busily to work timing the fastest horses he saw with his racing stop watch. He bought many horses on these speed records, despite my advice. He felt confident that he had come upon a miracle: the horses he had selected would win every event in every port city; their recorded gallops were faster than the records on any race course; and he knew China race courses well.

He stabled and fed his animals. Their coats took on a new glossy sheen. They even seemed to grow in size a little. Their teeth improved. But in the race tryouts their galloping speed was found to have dropped down to a level which made them no better and no worse than the average horse in China.

Another friend of mine, an Australian, pleased with the condition of his horses after six months of stable care and excellent grain-feeding, assured me that they were faster than any horses running uncared for in the Mongolian herds. He brought his horses up to the plateau again, with grooms to look after them, grain-feeding them all the way, attending carefully to their exercise, and making certain that they had plenty of water to drink. They looked lovely. They were sleekly groomed, and well fed in comparison with the shaggy horses on the plateau who had all their lives subsisted entirely on grass in a climate where grass is scarce more than six months of the year.

He generously offered good big prizes for any Mongol horses that could beat his in races. Courses were mapped out over which the races were to be run. The news spread far and wide. Horses began to come in from this state and that, straggling in every day until the date set for the competitive racing.

The Mongol owners admired the Australian's horses; they commented enviously upon the conditions of his life which made it possible for him to take such good care of his horses. Many of them remembered the animals, as I had bought them for him from the Mongolian herds. They stood other horses up alongside of them, to the Mongols' disadvantage. "They are beautiful, but can they run?" more than one man and woman asked.

The hour of the race came. Just as it was to start, still another Mongol came loping in over the hills. "Wait," the racers cried. "This is a good horse coming. He should have a try with the rest of us."

"He looks tired," my Australian friend said.

"A little," was the answer. "He has been taking part in the annual races held by the Prince of Durbit. He has done well. He won first place in the gelding race over a ten-mile course two days ago."

"What has he been doing since?"

The Mongols looked surprised, and someone answered: "He has been on the way here; it is a good many miles, and his rider has brought him as fast as he could. The news of your prize money traveled far. Never before in Mongolia have we been paid for winning races. It is wonderful. Heretofore our only recompense has been the sport and the prestige one got for winning."

This additional horse came in. He looked dusty, bedraggled, and tired. His head drooped and his tail hung listlessly. The horses were drawn up in a line for the race. Experienced jockeys who had come from China for the race rode the Australian's horses. I gave the signal. I expected to see the horses that had had every care imaginable during the past six months win easily. They were left behind in the first few furlongs. The horses who had never had veterinary attention, muscle-building grain, careful exercise, or shelter from cruel blizzards, left their competitors at their heels in the first start. Even the tired, dusty horse that had won a ten-mile race on one day and journeyed for two more to reach the place of this race stretched out, leaving the visitors enveloped in a cloud of dust. The horses that had covered themselves with glory on the China race course were defeated easily.

The horses that ran so far ahead of the visitors were no better horses than they. Many of them were not so good. A year earlier, before they had had such care, these beaten horses had won races in Mongolia, defeating the very horse that won first place on this day. When Mongol horses are stabled, the magic swiftness seems to drop from their legs.

Absolute freedom to run in the herd makes for real speed and entirely overbalances the advantages of civilization. My friend David Fraser, China correspondent for the London *Times*, has had most marvelous success in racing — not because the horses I have selected for him from Mongolia are peculiarly swift, but because he understands the needs of the horse that has been used to freedom. He keeps his horses' hoofs cut down to the size which was natural when they came from the plateau.

He hacks them many miles across country every day, trotting and cantering from Chinese village to Chinese village. Then when the racing season comes, his horses are hard and have kept in their limbs a goodly measure of that speed which was theirs on the Mongolian plain.

VII

CAMELS, CATTLE, SHEEP, AND GOATS

THE camel of Mongolia is the Bactrian camel, which has two humps. Almost every Mongolian family owns some camels; but all the breeding is done in the middle and western districts of the country, where there are large tracts of sandy land. From ancient times the camel has been the chief vehicle of transportation in this country.

Caravans of a thousand or more camels swing across the country to the borders of Turkestan, to Russia, or down through the Great Wall passes into China. They march from Inner to Outer Mongolia carrying goods from widely separated states. A caravan of camels seen at a distance often looks like a many-sailed ship outlined against the horizon. The Mongol puts a load up to four hundred English pounds on each pack animal. This is divided into two evenly weighted packs, one swung on either side of the camel's back. Loaded so, camels will travel day after day, feeding on whatever coarse shrubs and bushes there happen to be along the way, and going for long periods of time without water. They are very hardy and strong in cold weather, but the camel bred on the Mongolian plateau cannot bear summer heat. Therefore Mongolian caravans move in winter, early spring, or late autumn. If men do have to travel in summer, they go by night when it is cooler, and rest their animals during the day.

The camels are generally very gentle and docile, except in the breeding season, when they are really dangerous — especially the stallions. Then they are best left to run absolutely free and uncontrolled. Camels begin to mate about the fourth or fifth year. Males not wanted for breeding are castrated at three years. Camel mares drop their young only every other year.

The Mongols break their camels to the saddle when they are two years of age, and teach them to carry loads when they are five. Camels that are not overworked live to be about twenty.

In addition to breaking the camels to the saddle and the load, the Mongols of Northeastern Mongolia train their camels to draw carts. In this section freight is as often carried by cart as by pack. The carts are made with wheels placed far back, to minimize the shaking, as they are springless. The body of these carts is long enough for the Mongol riding on them to lie down at full length. Camels are also trained to carry a litter swung between two of them.

Mongolian camel breeders milk the camel mares. The milk is like thick cream and excellent in tea. It makes a rich cheese.

Camel wool is of very fine quality and is always in great demand. It is easily carded into yarn. Garments made of it are soft and light, yet exceedingly warm. Camels are not sheared, but every spring when the weather grows warm the thick wool comes loose from the hide and a gentle pull easily removes it from the body.

Camels are not very pretty when they have shed their wool, as they have a pink, delicate skin. The camel is at the lowest physical ebb at the moulting time. The new hair comes on slowly during the summer, growing thick and long when the cold sets in.

Camels are trained to lie down while their packs are loaded on, and to kneel when a rider desires to mount. They are guided by a single string tied to a little stick thrust through the nostrils. Camels in caravan go along in strings of ten, each tied by a nose string to the camel ahead. A man in front leads each group in the caravan.

Camels in caravan often wear out the soles of their feet. The Mongol then takes a piece of leather and sews on a patch, using rawhide string. This lasts but a few days, when he has again to patch the same place. If the camel can be turned free, the sole of the foot grows again, leaving no sign of the scar.

When camels are first taken from the summer grazing and put under the pack, they often stampede, scattering their burdens over the prairie. I have had this happen, my goods being flung far and wide, my camels, sometimes to the number of a hundred or more, dashing off madly toward the horizon. Stampeded camels are hard to overtake and bring back, and a stampede means a delay of several days. But after the camels have settled down to caravan work everything usually goes smoothly and well. They cover the miles at surprising speed.

THE AUTHOR MOUNTED ON A YOUNG RIDING CAMEL

I have always found that camels respond to petting. They are independent, haughty creatures until they have made friends with a man.

An angry camel is not a pleasant creature. When annoyed, he kicks out with a sudden, swift, sure aim. Dozens of times I have seen camels spit out the whole of a cud over a tormentor. It is a nasty, stinking mess which covers a man from head to foot. Furious camels have been known to bite off a man's arm, or to crush his face. Sometimes, if no help comes, they kill.

But the ordinary Mongol understands camels, and gets along peaceably with them. White camels are specially prized as riding animals. Camels are not as comfortable as horses to ride, but when one gets used to them they are not so bad. They provide the only means of travel across grassless waste land where a horse cannot live.

A young riding camel at a swift trot makes about the same speed as a galloping horse, and in long distances will outrun the horse. I had my first camel-riding experience when I went from residence under the patronage of the Prince of Ordos to spend my first year in Urga. The first day out the camel bucked me off, but I was not hurt. After this fall we settled down to friendly coöperation, and the camel carried me seventeen days across the Gobi peaceably.

The camel saddle ordinarily used is just a felt pad with stirrups of leather hanging down, one on either side. Lamas and wealthy men have saddles of similar pattern to those used on horses, with a high wooden pommel in front, padded seat, and silver stirrups.

Old women and children ride in baskets swung on either side of the camel. If there are two riders of nearly the same weight, they balance each other. When there is only one rider, the other side is balanced with a pack.

Cattle are not so plentiful in Mongolia as one might expect in a country of pasture land. The Mongols like milk, but they are not dependent upon the cow, because they get milk from the mare, the camel, the sheep, and the goat. All Mongols prefer mare's milk to cow's milk. When going on long journeys they carry cheese made from mare's milk, as it is more nourishing than that made from cow's milk.

The Mongols will eat beef, but they prefer mutton. A beef is too large an animal to kill, as they have no facilities for keeping the meat except in winter, when it freezes. The members of an encampment can easily dispose of a sheep at one time, so it is really more economical to provide themselves with mutton than with beef.

The oxen and the cows are used as pack and cart animals, but are not held in equal favor with camels. The cattle of Mongolia are a nondescript lot of various colors, and have unusually long horns. There is no selective breeding by the Mongols, but their cattle through the generations have developed these horns because they need them to fight off the wolves. Calves born without long horns lose their lives before they are old enough to pass on their characteristics.

A Mongol will have ten thousand horses and not consider that he has enough; but he will think his twenty cows plenty for any household. Of oxen he will keep just as many as he needs, to draw his carts when the camp moves, and no more.

The Mongol heifer usually calves in her fourth year. Male calves, except one for each herd, are castrated in their second year, and are broken to cart and pack the same summer.

Mongol cattle live a half-wild life. They are never stable-sheltered or stable-fed, and a great many die from cold and starvation every winter. The Mongol does nothing to safeguard their health. Rinderpest kills off large numbers of them. The only work that is being done to counteract this disease is by missionaries in South Mongolia and Russians in the north. They have done a great deal by introducing a vaccine against the disease, and have worked hard ever since I came here to interest the Mongols in cattle raising. Most foreigners believe the steppes should produce fewer horses and more cattle. This is wonderful cattle country, but the Mongols have little enthusiasm for cattle.

The Mongol cow all over the country is peculiar in that she will not give milk unless she has a calf. If a cow misses having a calf one year, she continues to suckle the calf of the year before, sometimes feeding an animal almost as large as herself.

If a calf is born and dies, the mother's milk dries up at once unless the Mongols do something to deceive her into thinking that her baby is still alive. It is the universal custom to stuff the dead calf's skin and prop it up against the cow each milking time. Then the milker milks with the calf held close against the cow while the mother licks and fondles it. Cows go off to graze every morning and leave their calves at the encampment, and they are accustomed to see them only at the milking time; consequently this ruse works surprisingly well. A cow will give milk until she has another calf if the stuffed body is presented to her each milk time.

At night cattle are tied up near the encampment. Horsehair ropes are pegged into the ground. The calves are tied to the inside rope and placed in rows facing each other, each calf fastened with a rope around its neck. In a rectangle around the calves, the cows are tied tightly with a noose looped over their horns. In a larger rectangle outside the cows, the steers are fastened. They are never tied very tightly, but left so that they can easily break loose and fight the wolves with their strong horns should any approach during the night.

The Mongols really live on their flocks of sheep. They furnish food, clothing, warm furs for floor padding, rugs to sleep in, and wool for felt to make tents.

The Mongol sheep is fairly large. Usually the males measure thirty to thirty-two inches, the females twenty to twenty-eight. A live male weighs seventy-two to one hundred and ten pounds, a female fifty-five to seventy-five. The head is high, and has strongly developed horns in the male. The nose is thin and bent, the legs long. The tail is fat — a well-developed storehouse in which, in the days when grass is plentiful, the sheep puts away a surplus for the long winter.

The sheep are white, often with black spots on head, neck, and flanks. They have thick, shaggy coats; the wool grows about six inches long. The Mongols shear twice during the summer, but a stomach band of two-inch-long wool is left on all except very strong, fat sheep. The wool makes very good felt, and a sheepskin coat is a splendid protection against cold. For knitted socks or any garment to be worn close to the body the Mongol prefers camel wool.

Sheep live to ten or twelve years of age in Mongolia; but sheep that have not proved good breeders or wool growers are used for mutton the seventh year. Mongolian mutton surpasses in tenderness and sweetness mutton I have eaten anywhere else in the world.

Breeding begins the second autumn. Ewes drop their young in February or March.

In summer the grass in Mongolia is so plentiful that the ewes have a large supply of milk. When there is more than enough to feed the lambs the Mongols use this milk too for making cheese. Sheep cannot be left untended, as even on the Mongolian plateau they have not developed the ability to shift for themselves as the horse has. They are run in flocks and herded by old men or children on horseback. The flock does not go far from home, and is brought back to the encampment every night and either folded in a corral or guarded by men and dogs between the yurtas. The lambs are cared for at home until they are quite big. In rainy weather they are housed in one of the felt yurtas.

Sheep thrive in Mongolia during the summer, but many flocks die in the winter blizzards. The Mongols have no facilities for feeding them, as they do not till the soil, and so produce no crops. The sheep have to forage for their food, summer and winter. They dig down under the snow for grass, but if a blizzard comes up when they are some distance from home it is almost impossible to get them back again. They huddle together motionless and are snowed under.

Traveling across the country one passes the skeletons of sheep which show just how they have piled up one on top of the other and died, several hundred of them in a heap.

Thousands of sheep are sold into China and Russia every year. There is always a demand for Mongolian sheepskin and wool.

Goats are fairly plentiful in Mongolia. They are always run mixed in with the sheep flocks. They give good milk, and their flesh also is eaten, although it does not have as nice a taste as mutton. Goatskins are used as rugs. There is a large demand for goatskins for export. Chinese traders go into Mongolia and buy all the skins available, which they bring down to Tientsin and export to foreign countries. The price of Mongolian goatskins has risen steadily for a long time, and has trebled in the past year.

VIII

POLITICAL HISTORY

MONGOLIA has a very long political history, but the Mongols are not a literary people. There are no records of their past except accounts written by people not native to the land and the folklore passed down by word of mouth from generation to generation. There are fragmentary historical documents dating from the ninth century on. All that I have ever seen up to the book on Marco Polo's seventeen-year visit to Kublai Khan in the thirteenth century are accounts of events written by political enemies of the Mongols — usually by literary men of countries defeated in war by the people of the plateau.

Since the beginning of history Mongolia has been the cradle of nomadic tribes which at various periods have shaken the foundations of the old civilized states of the Far East, the Near East, and Europe and reshaped their destinies. Mongolia remains important in world politics to-day, not only on account of her economic possibilities and resources, but more especially as the key to overland intercourse between the Far East and Europe.

The general impression of a stranger passing through Mongolia is that in military strength the country is hopelessly deficient, but in reality the strength of Mongolia in war is not so little as the casual observer might think. Every Mongol is a good horseman and an excellent shot. The entire population engages in hunting as sport. The Mongol shoots from the saddle, and he is accustomed from boyhood to take aim from the back of a galloping horse, either with the bow and arrow or with the lasso.

The bow and arrow was until recently the Mongol's chief weapon. Archery contests are still held annually in many states in Mongolia. Until the Soviet advisers came into power in North Mongolia, a thirty-day archery contest was held each year at Urga. Every state in Mongolia sent competitors. Tents were erected below the city — one group for nobles and one group for commoners.

During the first twenty-nine days the nobles contested against each other, and commoners also contested among themselves. Then, on the thirtieth day, the noble and the commoner who had been selected as the best of their respective groups met in an all-day contest. The winner was proclaimed the champion archer of Mongolia, and held the title for the year, when he had again to meet rivals in the same manner.

Archery targets are set up in the tournament grounds at different distances, none nearer than sixty steps. The archers are mounted on horseback and go full speed. Each shoots three arrows at three targets. The archer tries to place all three arrows in the three targets while his horse gallops at top speed! He is put to the trial many times in one day, aiming at targets on different sides of his horse, as well as in front of him and behind him. A surprising percentage of the tries are successful.

In addition to formal contests, Mongol men, priests and laymen, young boys, and even young girls, practise archery constantly. It is a fine sport for spirited people who enjoy playing games on horseback.

It takes a good eye and a steady hand to put an arrow into a target from the back of a galloping horse. The Mongols, bred as they are to accuracy with the arrow, are marvelous shots with the rifle, which they handle with surprising ease and learn to use with amazing quickness. A group of Mongol men, picked archers, armed with rifles and sent out to battle, rarely fail in bringing down a foe with each shot.

The Mongols love their land with a passion surpassing that of any other people I have ever met. In the defense of their own land they always have the advantage. They are used to the clear air and the high altitudes and can judge distances much more accurately than an outsider. The Mongol is clever in manœuvre, and skillful in luring his enemy out to where he can trap him.

The Mongols are possessed of unusual endurance and are able to go for long intervals of time without food or water and to stand exposure to weather. They are keen on physical fitness. Both lamas and laymen are hardened by frequent wrestling matches and by long daily gallops on the plateau.

Mongolian children are the product of generations inured to physical hardship. Parents here are too wise to soften their babes by coddling. When a child is weaned from his mother's milk and put on mare's milk he fends for himself. He eats when he is hungry from the available food — if there is any. He manages as best he can when caught in a storm. He is expected to pick up a stick and go after the wolves courageously if they approach. And he learns to ride as soon as he can walk. The place nearest the fire in the yurta belongs to the grown folk; boys and girls have to fit in where they can.

So with the food. All fare well in spring and summer, when horses and cows give lots of milk, sheep are fat, and game is abundant. In winter there is not so much to eat, and often there is a real scarcity. The able-bodied men have the first portion always; the women come next, and the children have what is left.

In addition to active resistance, the Mongols have a patient power of passive resistance even harder to conquer. They do not rush into battle. The population of Mongolia dwelling in yurtas can flit away by night. The herds can be driven off and the wells destroyed, so that the invader into Mongolia finds himself in a desert without food or water, where he is left to the mercy of nature.

Many things that have happened during my years in Mongolia have led me to the conviction that the Mongols are quite as able to hold their own against the foe as they were, according to historical records, in the days of Genghis Khan. My friendship with Prince Tochen Tachi has helped me to this conviction.

Tochen Tachi was originally a nobleman governing a very small state in Southeastern Mongolia. He was treacherously deprived of his homeland, which his ancestors had governed for many centuries, by Chinese land grabbers. While he was away from home the Chinese whom he had permitted to come into the state destroyed his royal yurtas, drove away his cattle, and murdered the women and children of his family, who had been left at home unprotected.

He swore vengeance against all Chinese, and left the home state. All of his tribe went with him. Their number was enlarged by other Mongols who had lost their loved ones and their yurtas in the same way. They swore an oath that they would harass and persecute every Chinese in Mongolia. They spread out into the country along the caravan routes, roaming into every place where a Chinese merchant happened to set up his tent. They took goods and life ruthlessly, leaving only a little pile of ashes to mark the place where a Chinese tent or cart had been. In this manner they made their way through all Eastern Mongolia, and then turned west toward Urga. Behind them lay a country cleared of Chinese.

The Mongols worked singly or in small groups. Tochen Tachi, with a few followers, pitched five yurtas beside a spring under the brow of a small hill and settled down within a few miles of Urga. In Urga there were several thousand Chinese merchants, and they trembled with fear. Tochen Tachi was a man with a few followers and they were thousands, but they were afraid that they would meet the same fate as their brother merchants in the country had done.

So the Chinese secured two hundred and fifty Chinese soldiers from the Chinese governor of Urga. Spies reconnoitred and reported that nearly all of Tachi's fellows were absent from his encampment. The Chinese soldiers made a wide detour round Tachi's yurtas, and the leaders of the attack took up a position just behind a hill overlooking the camp. At daybreak they opened fire on Tochen Tachi's yurtas and shot them absolutely to pieces.

Tochen Tachi, however, was far too clever to be caught by Chinese in his own country. He was not a careless man, and, as he told me afterwards, when the Chinese soldiers left Urga one of his own men also left Urga. This man rode faster and harder than the Chinese, and reported exactly how many soldiers were coming and how much ammunition they carried.

So the Mongols made deep dugouts inside their yurtas. Here they rested quite securely while the Chinese troops wasted all their ammunition in shooting tents to pieces. After the yurtas had collapsed, the Mongols jumped up with rifles in hand and began fighting in earnest from behind the débris of their tents. Every Mongol picked off a Chinese man. And while one half of the Mongol party fired away at the Chinese, Tochen and others ran to the wood where their horses stood saddled and bridled.

Tochen and each of his men had two cartridge belts and a rifle. They were dressed lightly so that they could run swiftly. He jumped on to his famous charger, the others leaped on to their horses, and they gave chase to the Chinese, who were already fleeing back toward Urga. The dare-devil Mongols tore after the Chinese at full speed. Tochen shot and killed a man with each cartridge in his two belts.

In telling me of this incident, Tochen Tachi concluded: "My men had all done well. I considered it a day's work. We thought we needed food and rest. We rode to the place where we had other tents pitched."

The story of this deed spread into Urga, with many other legends of the nobleman's exploits. The Living Buddha, then Emperor of Mongolia, sent for him. Tochen Tachi was appointed to an official position in the Ministry of War, where he has served loyally.

Lama priests, as well as laymen, make good soldiers. The Incarnate Lama of Karasha, in addition to being the religious leader of his territory, has under his generalship a large and well-drilled army of Mongolian soldiers. His men are equipped with modern arms and ammunition, and their training includes all the Mongol methods of increasing a man's powers of endurance and sharpening his eyesight, with additional education in Western tactics and the use of Western military materials. He has several thousand men who could be called upon in an instant to right a Mongol wrong.

Mongolia is a table-land, occupying one million, three hundred and seventy thousand square miles in the heart of the Asiatic continent. It is bounded by Russia and China, and serves as a buffer state between these countries. Each is eager to keep it a buffer state.

The size of Mongolia and the difficulty of transporting an army across it stand in the way of war between China and Russia. Russia and China vie with each other for Mongolian favor; politically and materially, Mongolia interests both of them. Both countries depend on Mongolia for beef and mutton; both need the Mongolian horse for farm and military use.

Mongolia is a land of rich virgin soil, sparsely populated. Russia and China are united in being alert against the danger of overpopulated Japan cultivating a friendship here and finding an outlet for expansion.

Folklore tells that the Mongol race came into being by will of the great God. All the heroes and heroines of Mongolia, from the dim past through the centuries to the present day, are always spoken of as *bogda* — that is, "of the race of gods."

In the tents at eventide, on caravan trips, at the summer festivals, during wedding celebrations, or on other occasions when folk have time for song and story, they tell their history in mythical language, regardless of whether the event is of the same day or of ages past. They think of life as bound up in forces too great to explain. Nothing is impossible. From their tales one can patch together a history (which tallies with the written records of the Uigurs, the Chinese, the Persians, the Armenians, the Venetians, and the Russians) down to 1893, when I came to live here.

Early Chinese accounts describe a race who resembled the Mongols in habits and appearance.

They call them the Hsiung-nu, and speak of their occupying territory which corresponds to the present-day location of Mongolia. An account put down early in the reign of Kao Ti, the founder of the Han dynasty in China in 206 B. C., says that he chose Changan in Shensi for the location of his capital because he desired a position from which he could watch the movements of the wild Hsiung-nu. The record describes the Hsiung-nu as a people who, when asked where their home was, replied, "On the backs of our horses." It states that even their babies rode on sheep and shot birds with little bows and arrows; that they fed on cheese made from mare's milk; that they had camels as beasts of burden to carry their houses, which folded up like umbrellas; and that they frequently swept down from the plateau into China, killing many people and carrying off large quantities of valuable things. The account complains of the annual subsidy of silks, rice, wine, and beautiful maidens that had to be given to keep them from devastating all North China.

Memoranda of incessant trouble between the Chinese and the plateau people lead up to the chieftain Liu Yuan, who in the third century A. D. entered China with fifty thousand warriors on horseback and took into captivity the second emperor of the Tsin dynasty. After him, his brother carried the third and the fourth Tsin emperors into captivity on the plateau. Then the Hsiung-nu reigned supreme in North China for sixty years. They placed their capital near the present site of Peking and styled themselves the "sons of Heaven."

Western records of 445 A. D. tell of the invasion of
Europe by the Huns. As they are described these
Huns are so similar to the Mongols of to-day that
they appear to be their ancestors, even without
the additional testimony of Mongolian folklore,
which chants of this sally into Europe "before the
hour of Genghis Khan."

A Chinese writer in 1125 A. D. tells of the warriors
from the northern plateau who captured Kaifeng,
the capital of the Sungs. Translated literally, his
account is as follows:—

"They fight on horseback. Their forces are divided
into companies of fifty men. In each company
twenty men wearing cuirasses and carrying short
swords and pikes make up the front rank. The remaining thirty make the rear rank; they wear lighter
armor and are armed with bows and arrows and
javelins. In battle they all advance at a trot until
within a hundred yards of us; then their horses come
at a swift gallop. The riders guide their mounts
miraculously without rein and have both hands
free to use their weapons. After they have discharged
their arrows they retire with celerity. These tactics
are repeated several times before they fall upon
us with sword and pike."

To-day the people of the plateau sing of Genghis
as one of the mighty gods. There are ample authentic
records of his genius. He was born after the middle
of the twelfth century and was left heir to the chieftainship of his tribe by the death of his father in his
thirteenth year. But the tribe refused at first to
acknowledge his leadership. He was tempered in

the furnace of adversity through all his youth, and after incessant battles with nature, with himself, and with his fellow plainsfolk he was proclaimed Most Mighty Khan in his forty-fourth year, with all the tribes of the plateau united under him in a confederacy of Mongols — "Mongol" meaning brave man. With him at their head the Mongols made themselves masters of every country they entered. They drew up a code of laws which they enforced from Korea to the further banks of the Volga, from Turkestan to the Caspian.

The Mongols were still in the mood of curiosity concerning the outside world when Genghis "returned to the gods." Under the emperorship of his succeeding son, Ogotai, they not only enforced their will on the vast realm he inherited, but swept out in further conquest. They defeated Jelal ed-Tin and brought Armenia under their banner, subdued all China within the eastern bend of the Yellow River, pressed on to the Adriatic, destroyed Moscow, and burned the Russian imperial family in the Cathedral of Vladimir. They came to the gates of Vienna, penetrated Korea, humbled Southern Persia, and invaded Poland.

On the death of Ogotai domestic dissension as to who should succeed him occupied the Mongols for ten years. Then Kublai, favorite grandson of Genghis and child of Ogotai's brother Tuli, was unanimously proclaimed Khan.

During the khanship of Kublai, the third and longest wave of the Mongols' conquest rolled out from the plateau. They rode over Mesopotamia, crushed the kalifates and made Bagdad and Damascus their own, galloping near to Jerusalem. They flew their ensign, the oxtail, over Antioch, entered Asia Minor as far as Smyrna, and went within a week's march of Constantinople. They overthrew the Sung dynasty and extended their dominion over China to the borders of Malay. They forced their law on Tibet, on Annam, and on Burma.

In 1260 A. D. Kublai Khan caused a golden city to be made ready as his capital in North China. This city was called Cambaluc and is now known as Peking. It was not built in the style of Chinese cities, with narrow twisting streets, but with long wide roads through which horsemen can gallop nine abreast. Kublai Khan gave his Chinese dynasty the name "Yuan," which means "original."

By their own written testimony, the Chinese enjoyed an extraordinary prosperity under Mongol rule, just as they always prosper when a strong man keeps peace in their land. Trade and industry flourished. Their alien ruler took rich tribute to maintain a gorgeous court; they were proud of the magnificence and the pageantry of his reign.

He ordered roads made and established a pony-express postal service; he caused the reconstruction of the Imperial Grand Canal between Hangchow and Tientsin, which is a thousand miles long and still forms one of the chief means of inland transportation in China.

Kublai Khan was sovereign over a territory larger than that of any other ruler known to history. He governed by peaceful means, once he had conquered.

In this he had the teaching and the example of his father and of his grandfather. Casual students are prone to call his grandfather Genghis "the Scourge of God," neglecting to note that he gave to his world a wise code of laws so usable that they are still the base of justice in Mongolia to-day. And the Mongols dwell in peace with each other.

Under the Mongol overlordship the world had an era of peace. When these superior warriors conquered, all petty warfare came to an end. The pattern of civilization was altered and many people perished; but those who survived lived in a Renaissance. The blood feuds of the Russian princes were blotted from the pages of history. Mohammedanism was checked. Western scientists and artisans were brought into the Far East by the Mongol conquerors; Far Eastern culture and administrative ability penetrated the West.

China was united for the first time. Her scholars, basking in the soft air of peace, produced a wealth of literature and made the century notable for its written drama. The gardens of the scholars of Islam were wrecked by the incoming conquerors; but nature is possessed of an inexhaustible power of new growth: roses soon bloomed on the ruins, and the tearing away of old foliage let light into the minds of the scholars.

The breaking down of the national boundaries and the amalgamation of half the world into one well-governed unit made travel over a vast area possible, for the first time in history. The Mongols kept open roads through all their realm. Along the roads passed a continuous pageant of travelers. Christians journeyed safely to visit the Holy Sepulchre; Mohammedans went in peace to the Temple of Solomon. Hindu priests from Burma and Catholic priests from Venice came to North Asia. An interest in the world stirred in the breasts of people who had been content to rest in narrow-minded ignorance of any civilization other than their own. Persian princes, Korean magicians, Turkish gentlemen, Russian nobles, and Venetian traders mingled with red-hat lamas from Tibet, artisans from Smyrna, and crusaders from Antioch, and met the Chinese sage named Ye Lui Chutsai at the court of the Mongol khans.

Although mercilessly cruel in the hour of conquest, there is ample evidence in folklore and in written statement that the Mongol overlords enforced the rule of religious freedom for all when they settled down to administer the government. There is a tale often told to Mongolian children: "And one day, when Ogotai was the Great Khan, a man who professed to be a follower of Buddha's teaching, but who had not learned the definition of universal love, came to him saying: 'The spirit of your father Genghis came to me in the night. He commanded me to deliver a message to you. He bids you exterminate all believers in Mohammed, as they are fester spots on earth and infect other men with mental sickness.'

"The Great Khan made answer: 'Did my father address you by an interpreter?'

"'His ghost spoke to me direct.'

"The Khan smiled: 'And thou knowest the Mongol way of speech?'

"The man hung his head, as it was known through all the camp that he spoke in a queer foreign tongue and must address all Mongols through an interpreter. 'Thou knowest, Great Khan, that I cannot speak Mongol.'

"'Ah,' Ogotai answered in evident relief, 'then thou hast mistook thy ghost. My father knew no tongue except Mongol.' And the wise Khan continued to permit all men to find God in their own way."

Among the commands sent by Kublai Khan to his vassal states was an order that all Christians were to be freed from unequal servitude and taxes and to be treated with honor and reverence. And when Hulagu, the grandson of Genghis, represented his cousin Kublai as administrator of Syria he issued an edict to the effect that every religious sect should proclaim its faith openly and would have protection from the government if molested by the followers of another faith.

The Mongols never hoarded treasures. To judge by accounts, they were always as careless of material wealth as they are to-day. They like beautiful things, especially jewels or silks of gay color, but except for desiring great herds of horses they have no eagerness for possession. They are lavish in gifts to friends and generous in charity to folk who by misfortune are without necessities. "If a neighbor has no horse and I have two, then it is only sensible that he should have one of them. A man can take nothing with him when he leaves this world." That is the philosophy I hear continually.

Genghis Khan sneered at the treasures amassed by the monarchs he conquered. It is written that he prodded a bag of gold contemptuously with his boot and said: "Fools! This did them no good. They took nothing out with them when we killed them." He and his followers ruthlessly destroyed the material treasures found in the lands they conquered, taking only a small portion back to the plateau.

The great khans liked gorgeous, colorful decorations for their tents, their mounts, and their persons. All Mongols still do, but they have no tendency to hoard even jewels away in hidden chests. I have a friend who has seven glorious emeralds, handed down from the days of conquest. She wears them in a band in her hair even when she is milking.

Kublai Khan, according to Marco Polo and others, lived in a state of rich pageantry, but he stored away no secret fortune. When Ogotai was admonished for giving away lavish presents to everyone he met, — once a string of pearls to a beggar woman, — he replied: "I shall soon be gone from the earth. Then my only abiding place will be in the memory of people." Longfellow, the American poet, has immortalized this philosophy with splendid verses in which he tells the tale of the meeting of Hulagu, grandson of Genghis, and the Kalif of Bagdad, in the thirteenth century: —

"I said to the Kalif, 'Thou art old;
Thou hast no need of so much gold.
Thou shouldst not have heaped and hidden it here
Till the breath of battle was hot and near.'"

The Mongol world rule dissolved almost as quickly as it was created. The Mongols chant that none of their women were so foolish as to leave the glorious free nomad life on the beautiful plateau and that the men soon sickened of the stagnant air of foreign places and came home again — for although they found good salt in battle, the taste of the conquered world was insipid in days of idle peace.

Kublai died in 1294. He was succeeded by his grandson Temur — "a man grown too soft by a childhood in China," so the Mongols say. Temur was followed by several China-bred descendants, but by 1368 the Mongols had returned north of the Wall.

Ghazan followed Hulagu in administration in the Near East, but he sent few reports to his second cousin Temur, and neglected to attend his coronation. He died abroad, and was succeeded by descendants only half Mongol, who by intermarriage were absorbed into this far country. No fresh Mongol blood went out to administer the law in distant lands after the death of Kublai.

In 1400 the last remnants of the Mongols, mixed descendants of Batu the son of Juchi, who was the first-born son of Genghis, had become so weakened that they lost their governmental power in South Central Asia and Persia to Tamerlane, the Turk.

In 1555 Ivan the Terrible of Russia easily shook the Mongol dictatorship from Russia. But it was not until midway in the eighteenth century that the Mongols entirely let go of their hold on the

outside world. Six centuries after its conquest by
Genghis his scions gave Hindustan over to British
rule. But long before this thousands of exiled Mongols
had come back to their homeland.

Temur, the grandson of Kublai Khan, lived in
China. He was too weak a man to hold the Mongol
homeland as a unit. Numerous men stronger than
himself assumed leadership in various places, and
the government was broken up into groups as in the
days before Genghis amalgamated the people of the
plateau into one invincible band. This division into
groups continued for nearly a hundred years, until
1470, when there appeared a Mongol strong enough
to reunite them. His name was Dayan. He was not
concerned with any territory beyond the borders
of the plateau, but during his days Mongolia enjoyed a golden era.

Dayan was a wise man. Mongol folk tales are
rich in stories about him. They sing that he lived
for a hundred years. The Chinese record that he
died in 1544. He left eleven sons behind him when
he went from the earth. They were unable to come
to a unanimous decision as to which one of them
should succeed him, so the plateau was broken up
into eleven states, each governed by an independent
monarch.

During the Ming rule in China the Mongol chieftains harried that country sorely, frequently swoop-
ing down and making raids within the Wall, as they
had done through the centuries since the beginning
of recorded Chinese history. One account tells how,
in the middle of the fifteenth century, a leader of a

Chinese army induced the Emperor Ying Tsung to accompany an expedition against the Mongols, with the thought that his presence would inspire the troops.

This army was almost completely annihilated. The general was killed, and the Emperor taken to Mongolia and held for a high ransom. This battle occurred near the city of T'u Muh. I pass this city every time I go from Mongolia to Peking by horseback. Its walls are still scarred by the stone cannons the Mongols used in that battle, and its people still tell in folklore of that siege of T'u Muh.

These raids continued until finally, early in the seventeenth century, the descendants of the sons of Dayan, who were monarchs of the states of the plateau south of the Gobi, joined with the Tartar clans of Manchuria, under the leadership of a prince called Nurhachu, in a serious invasion of China.

Nurhachu, with a force of forty thousand men, set out for China in 1618. He met the Chinese first at Liaotung, and completely routed them. The Tartars fought on to Moukden and established a capital there in 1625. Nurhachu died in 1627, and was succeeded by his son T'ai Tshung.

T'ai Tshung, with an army now grown to a hundred thousand Tartars, marched into China and camped not far from Peking. The Tartars were unable to take the capital this time, and had to retire behind the Wall.

Shortly after this T'ai Tshung died, and left as his successor a small son, with a Tartar prince named Durgan as regent. In 1644 Prince Durgan led the

Tartars into China again. At this time China was so weakened by civil war that the Tartars had no difficulty in capturing the Ming throne and proclaiming the little Tartar prince, Shun Chih, grandson of Nurhachu, Emperor of China.

This marked the beginning of an era of peace, such as the peace of the Yuan dynasty, between China and Mongolia. Nurhachu and his descendants were of the Tartar tribe called Manchus, but sprouts of the same original root as the Mongols. They called their dynasty the Ch'ing, which means "pure."

The Mongol rulers of the plateau states bordering on Manchuria and China had helped in this conquest. They pledged their allegiance to the new dynasty and received innumerable privileges, such as the right to collect revenues at certain gates in China, which rights they held until the end of the Manchu rule.

Mongolia continued to be split up into smaller and smaller states in a division of territories among the sons of rulers until early in the eighteenth century. Then there rose a chieftain, Tse Ling, who united the tribes again under one head government. He continued in peace with the Manchus; he did not attempt to interfere with the inherited rights in China of the chieftains under him. He died in 1745, and was succeeded by his son Dardsha.

Dardsha was slain by his jealous cousin, Amursama. Amursama proclaimed himself ruler of all Mongolia. But another cousin, Dayatsi, who had urged Amursama to kill Dardsha, coveted the chieftainship for himself. These two fell to quarreling and Amursama ran to the Manchu court. He was cordially welcomed at Peking. The Manchu emperor Ch'ien Lung gave him ammunition and food supplies and a large Manchu army. With this help Amursama soon put an end to his cousin Dayatsi and proclaimed himself chieftain of all the Mongols. At the same time he pledged himself an obedient vassal to his Manchu relative, the Emperor of China.

But as soon as Amursama felt himself secure in Mongolia he repudiated his pledges to the Manchus and instigated raids into the rich Chinese territory south of the Great Wall. Ch'ien Lung then dispatched a powerful expedition against him, and Amursama fled to Russia, where he shortly afterwards died.

At the time of the trouble between Dayatsi and Amursama the Mongolian tribe known as the Turguts were so disgusted that they accepted the invitation of the Russian Government to go and settle in the rich pasture valleys of the Volga. They dwelt there for half a century; but Mongols are never happy or healthy away from their own plateau, and in the winter of 1771 they took down their yurtas and began a long and perilous journey home. De Quincey, in his book, *The Flight of a Tartar Tribe*, depicts this host of one hundred and sixty thousand men, women, and children in their trek across Russia. The Russians tried to arrest their departure, but Mongols and Manchus went to meet them, and after eight months of terrific hardship more than half their number reached the shores of their loved Lake Tengis again.

The Mongol tribes never accepted Amursama as

their chieftain. He had no power over a united Mongolia even in the days when he proclaimed himself monarch and pledged his country in vassalage to the Emperor of China. The country broke up into innumerable minor states on the death of Dardsha, each governed by a ruler who gave no allegiance to the central power.

The raids on China led by the treacherous Amursama made the Manchus uneasy concerning their ability to hold the Chinese throne if all the Mongol tribes should turn against them; so the Emperor gave thought to the strength of his frontier. He attended to the Great Wall fortifications on the plateau border; he sent out an expeditionary army and annexed Eastern Turkestan; and he made Jehol, a position from which he could cultivate friendships with the Mongol chieftains, the Manchu summer capital.

From now on during their rule the Manchus sought to develop a close relationship with the Mongols of the plateau. They encouraged the marriage of Mongol rulers and Manchu princesses, and conferred titles and special privileges in China on all Mongols. They invited the Mongols to enter into all the festivities of the Chinese court, giving them precedence over the Chinese. Through their Manchu wives, the nomad princes were encouraged to build and keep up expensive establishments in Peking. The Manchus fostered the religious bent of the Mongols towards Lamaism, considering that it would deplete their martial virility.

The Manchus' policy of government in China was

conciliatory during the whole of their rule. The Tartar prince Durgan, who was regent for the infant Prince Shun Chih at the time of the foundation of the dynasty, revived and adopted many ancient Chinese customs and terms which had been neglected by the Mings.

The Manchu emperors made annual reports of government business to Heaven from an outdoor amphitheatre, in the manner of the early Chinese emperors of mythical history; they favored Confucianism; they selected officials to assist in their government from among their Chinese subjects by Chinese literary examinations; and they permitted Chinese farmers to enter Manchuria.

Up to 1644, the beginning of the Manchu occupancy of the Chinese throne, no Chinese were permitted to pass beyond the Great Wall. Immediately after, thousands of Chinese farmers swarmed out to till the rich virgin soil of the Manchu homeland which had previously been used only by the grazing herds of nomad tribes.

Once the Chinese had spread beyond the Great Wall, it was not so easy to keep them out of Mongolia. They coveted the right to cultivate the plateau, judging from its luxuriant growth of grass that it was fertile.

The Manchus dropped their nomad habits when they became rulers of China. They grew fond of varied and delicate foods and went physically soft in stone houses that kept out cold and heat. As their physical endurance weakened their fear of their Mongol cousins grew; so they made every effort to weaken the Mongols too. They sent Chinese merchants on to the plateau to friendly princes, tempting the Mongols to eat alien food and to desire weakening luxuries. They persuaded the rulers of the territory around the summer capital, Jehol, to let the Chinese "slaves" toil in producing foreign delicacies for imperial feasts, saying to the Mongols that there could be no possible harm in this migration of farmers, as the blindest man could see the Chinese were cowards in temperament.

So the Chinese penetrated into the plateau as traveling merchants and took root as tillers of the soil on the Mongolian border; and the Manchus pressed this advantage by suggesting that they supply officials to keep the Chinese in order, lest they slyly usurp power.

Even during my boyhood in the country in Sweden I was keenly interested in the Mongols. I procured every book about them I could, and added to my collection when I went to study in England. When I came to the Far East first I lived in Paotow in North China, and I used to ask innumerable questions concerning the government of the Mongolian people from the Manchu official in Paotow, who became my friend.

My books and my Manchu friend taught me that Mongolia was a vassal state of China, and explained in detail how the plateau was divided up into neat political sections, compact and orderly, each section administered by a governor from Peking.

Then I went to live under the patronage of the

Mongol Prince of Ordos. During my three months with him I began to wonder if there was treachery in the state of Ordos and to expect trouble; but no trouble ever occurred, despite the high-handed, independent way in which the Prince ruled his state.

From Ordos I went to Urga, where I met a great many Mongolian princes. In the next few years I visited almost every state in Mongolia. I found that the independence of each state depended entirely upon the strength of the man who happened to be the ruler.

Many of these Mongol princes had Manchu wives. But as I visited various royal palaces I learned that there was almost always a Mongol wife also, dwelling in a royal yurta a little way outside the palace. The women of these yurtas reared their children in the same way as the Mongol children have been reared for centuries.

The Manchu wife, never happy on a plain, was always eager to go on a visit to China and to take her children with her. The Mongol wife handled the state affairs when her husband went with the Manchu to Peking, and her children early took a grip on state management. Few of the Mongol-Manchu offspring survived the rigors of life on the plateau, and in nearly every state in Mongolia today it is a pure-bred son who sits on the throne of his father. These sons of the Mongol wives were not softened or corrupted by the life at the Manchu court. It takes a strong man to survive as a Mongol monarch, and a strong man to seize and hold the throne when his father dies.

The Manchus at the time they conquered China were a hard-riding, iron-sinewed people, but they deteriorated as a result of three centuries of life in China. They took their women with them into China, and although they kept their blood pure by a law which forbade marriage with a Chinese, they gave their homeland, Manchuria, over to Chinese cultivation and kept no place in which to continue to breed physical hardiness as the Mongols did when they ruled China during the Yuan dynasty.

The officials who were sent into Mongolia to hold positions that were marked on papers by the Chinese as governmentships were never really comfortable on the plateau. Most of them were quite content to reside in the border towns. The Mongol princes invited them to their summer festivals, but beyond that they took no part in the life of the plateau, so far as I know. I never met a Chinese official at a wolf hunt or an archery contest, or on any expedition which meant a test of endurance.

Presumably these officials looked after the Chinese traders in Mongolia, but in reality they seldom interfered with a Mongol prince if he ordered the traders out of his state entirely. The Chinese governor resident at Urga used to drive each afternoon in a covered cart. For the rest of the time he dwelt quietly within his own walls.

The Mongols never made any attempt to refute the stories of their subjugation by the Chinese which are circulated about them — primarily, I think, because the stories do not interest them.

Things went on like this until 1910, with everything

quite peaceful on the plateau. The Manchus and the Mongols understood each other perfectly. The Manchus realized their weakening power and were eager to keep the Mongols their friends. The Mongols looked on the weakened Manchus with mingled contempt and pity for the way in which they had lost their ancestral strength and vigor.

But in 1910 a young Chinese governor named San To was sent to Urga. He was a man more energetic than wise, and he adopted a very forward policy. He ordered barracks built for a division of Chinese troops, and Chinese military officers arrived in Urga in preparation for the enforcement of the paper rule of Mongolia. Following the military officers there came an immigration of Chinese colonists and their wives.

There were several thousand traders in Urga and scattered throughout the country, but the traders were not permitted to bring their wives, and in many states had to move their tents every twenty-four hours. The Mongols considered the coming of these colonists a very different matter from the entry of Chinese traders into Mongolia. San To went a step further and sent an order to the Mongol princes in which he took them to task over their friendly relations with Russia.

The princes were not pleased with this man. The Prince of Hanta, particularly, felt that he should go back beyond the Great Wall where he belonged. As other Mongol noblemen did not at first treat the matter as seriously as the Prince of Hanta, he showed his disgust by leaving the capital city and going back into his own state. There he got together his own state soldiers, and then returned to Urga and drove the Manchus out. This revolution was a bloodless revolution, all accomplished in a few hours overnight. Mongol soldiers led by the Prince of Hanta very quickly disarmed the sleeping Manchu soldiers, and in the early morning the Mongolian people woke to know themselves a people free from Chinese interference.

I was in Urga at the time. Both the Living Buddha and the Prince of Hanta sent me word sometime after sunset that if I heard any disturbance in the night I was not to worry but to stay in bed. I heard nothing, and was quite surprised in the morning to hear that there were no more Manchu soldiers or officials in Urga. The whole thing gave me a very high opinion of the Mongols, because there was no bloodshed, and no looting in the Chinese quarter of Urga.

The Manchu governor and his attendant officials were treated well, even respectfully. They were sent in their own carriages over the Russian border with a safety escort of Mongol soldiers. From there they could easily make their way by train and boat down to Peking. The Chinese soldiers were sent overland to Kalgan. Each soldier was provided with a good camel and with a pass which assured him plenty of food along the way. The Chinese were allowed to take all their own private property, including their riding ponies.

News of the revolution was brought to me before I was up. I dressed and went at once to the telegraph office to send a wire to my wife in China so that she would not be alarmed by any reports which came to her. The operator in the telegraph office was a Chinese. I filled out my telegraph blank and handed it to him. He said: "I cannot possibly transmit the word 'revolution.' That is a very bad word — a very bad word indeed."

A Mongol hunter who happened to hear this conversation spoke. "It goes," he said, looking at the clerk seriously.

The poor clerk trembled.

It went.

Since the treachery of Amursama there had been no man in Mongolia to amalgamate the independent tribes into one strong unit. The Mongols felt that, while they did very well with states governed independently, they needed to put up a united front to the outside world. The Mongol princes met and discussed the matter. The most popular man in Mongolia at this time was the Living Buddha. They unanimously decided to ask him to become Emperor. I have described the ceremonies of his coronation in an earlier chapter.

About this same time the Manchus were forced to abdicate their throne to China. The Chinese Republican Government tried to hold on to all outlying territory, but in January 1912 Barga decided to separate from China and become a part of the Mongolian Empire. In the same year the territories from Uliassutai to Kobdo requested to come under the Living Buddha's emperorship. On

November 3, 1912, the Emperor of Mongolia exchanged agreement papers with Russia in which Russia promised aid, if needed, in preserving Mongolia from Chinese colonization, and Mongolia promised Russia a continuation of trade privileges and notification in case of entering into any treaty with a foreign power.

By this time the Chinese had practically all left the north of Mongolia, but the presence of the numerous colonists on the southern border irritated the Mongols. The Chinese had been pressing in a little farther and a little farther ever since the Manchus permitted them to cross the Great Wall into their own territory.

The Mongols resented this colonization, but they did not take action concerning it until China, made audacious by her quick success in the upsetting of the Manchu throne and the establishment of the Republic, sent an army into Mongolia to subjugate Southern Mongolia and capture more of this fertile territory for her farmers.

In 1913 war started on the border simultaneously in Ulanchap, Chaharm Silingol, and the northern Chou-Uda. When the Chinese army marched into Mongolia, the Mongols encircled it and hid in a ravine or under the brow of a hill, waited in concealment until the Chinese had all passed them, and then rode out and attacked the army's flank. Such battles were over almost as soon as they were begun. Almost every one of the Mongol's bullets brought down a Chinese man, and soon there was a stampede of the Chinese cavalry.

The Chinese army were entering a strange country. They had to follow the road of the trade route, where they knew that there were wells so that they could camp and water and feed men and beasts. The Mongols knew every inch of the ground. They were here one day and there the next, flitting about so that it was impossible for the Chinese generals even to guess where their foes were.

A favorite trick of the Mongols was to wait until the Chinese had camped for the night, giving them plenty of time to settle down to sleep. Then at midnight the Mongols would begin to annoy the camp, sniping down a guard here and another one there a few minutes later, directing a bullet into this tent, dropping another one into that, and making the Chinese so nervous that they would start their machine guns and their rifles. Then when the Mongols attacked in the morning in earnest the Chinese would be tired and much of their ammunition would have been wasted.

The Chinese army had difficulty in getting any ammunition except that which they carried right with them. Transport supplies had to have with them a strong guard, but even then the Mongols usually managed to capture the transport caravan.

I once asked the Mongolian Minister of War how he dared send Mongol men out across the Gobi Desert to fight the Chinese on the border with only such ammunition as each man could carry on his person. He answered: "Each of these lads is supposed to have a rifle and a cartridge belt, but we don't have enough to go round. Still, I don't worry —

I know that every one of these men will come back with more rifles and ammunition than he started out with."

This prophecy proved true. During this war I continually met caravans coming away from the places of battle loaded with guns and ammunition taken from the enemy. The Mongol who has to go out to battle without a rifle uses his wits to collect one as soon as possible.

Lamas and laymen were equally keen in clearing out the Chinese. Muronga was a lama priest who fought valiantly for Mongolia in the war of 1913 against China. He was a very religious priest in all outward form — a priest who spent the greater part of his time in his yurta reading prayers and counting his rosary. From his yurta, though, he directed the activities of the soldiers, who looked upon him as their leader. He had gathered about him a band of ruthless, embittered men who never hesitated to take life either in battle or in peaceful encounter. Their motto was an avowed hatred against the Chinese.

Muronga lost his life because he carried his hatred of the Chinese so far that he killed Mr. Grant, an Englishman. Mr. Grant was an employee of the Chinese Telegraph Service, and was traveling from Pang King, the most southern telegraph station in Mongolia, with several Chinese who had been entrusted to his care as far as Kalgan. While still on the Mongolian plateau, Grant and his party met three mounted men, who forced them to leave the road and go into their camp. Muronga had his headquarters in this camp. He spoke to the English-man and told him that he could go on quietly to Kalgan, as nothing was desired of him, but that he must leave his Chinese companions in the Mongolian camp. They were to be killed as soon as he had ridden away.

Grant replied that the Mongols would have to kill him first if they were going to kill the Chinese, as he had promised to escort them safely to Kalgan.

Grant was taken at his word — he was shot first and all the Chinese after him. With the help of my Mongol friend I went to see Muronga and received from him Mr. Grant's remains, which I took to Peking.

Muronga was ordered to Urga. He refused to go. So a general was sent from North Mongolia with soldiers. Muronga was arrested. According to Mongolian common law — one of the original regulations which have come down from the days of Genghis Khan — a Mongol may not spill the blood of a Mongol nobleman or priest. So Muronga was sewed up in a felt and put on a camel. He was shaken to death long before he arrived at Urga.

During this war between Mongolia and China I went to spend the summer with my family at my ranch at Tabo-Ol, which is on the plateau, about ninety miles north of Kalgan.

Yuan Shih-Kai, the then ruler of China, sent an official up from Peking and asked me to make peace between China and Mongolia. I believed that the war was destructive to both countries, and so under-took to do what I could.

My Mongolian friends were in no mood to assist me. The Mongols who were doing the active fighting against China on the Chahar border were Mongols from Northeast Mongolia. I had no friends among the military leaders. I went to Urga and tried to induce the Emperor to make peace, but was not successful in securing any order for hostilities to stop. I decided that the only thing to do was to go to the headquarters of the Mongols who were leading the trouble. I learned that they were established at a Mongol temple.

When I was still some distance from this temple, I encountered two guards. After some talk they agreed to escort me to headquarters. When I arrived at the temple I had hardly time to dismount from my horse before I was surrounded by thirty or forty men. They stood in a menacing circle with their fingers on the triggers of Mauser pistols. It all struck me as quite funny, and I broke into a hearty laugh. They stared at me as though I were mad. When I had recovered myself, I asked them if they had considered that if they all started shooting at one time it was certain that every bullet that did not embed itself in bone in my body would go through me and kill a comrade on the opposite side of the circle. I suggested that if they all stood on my side they could finish me off without any hurt to themselves. They saw my point, and broke the circle at once. This movement gave me time to ask some of them to take me to their leader on important business.

There was argument as to whether my business was really important, but eventually two of them went off and saw Prince Na. They soon came back. They were now very polite to me, and conducted me at once to the best house of the temple, in which house Prince Na had his offices and sleeping quarters. He greeted me, and after the usual formal phrases I told him that I was both hungry and thirsty. Hospitality is the common-law courtesy in Mongolia; food and drink must be given to every guest.

Prince Na ordered tea and cheese for me. It was brought quickly. The parley over, the tea gave me time to talk to him. I told him that I had come on a serious errand, but preferred to talk to him more in private — the house was by that time filled with men who pressed close about us.

Prince Na understood me, and said: "As you have now arrived and are with me, the business is not so pressing. You must first take time for refreshment. I have ordered a good dinner prepared for you, and until it is ready you must rest."

The dinner took some time to prepare, but as soon as it came in I knew that I was all right. The meal was the fat tail together with the back of a sheep, boiled whole, and was handed to me on an immense brass platter laid on the widespread palms of two hands. In Mongolia the giving of such food is a sign that the house entertains an honored guest in peace. In my early days in Mongolia I found this kind of food very difficult to eat on account of the great amount of fat, but by now I had learned to cut out the dark, tender meat from the backbone.

I ate of this meat, which is good and sweet, and felt quite satisfied at the end of my meal. It was quite late by this time, and Prince Na said that we must now go to bed. He took me with him into his own bedroom. This was a room in the temple built in Chinese fashion, with a wide stone bed built against the wall.

When I was inside the room, Prince Na gave sharp instructions to a couple of strong young men to guard our door during the night. After that he locked the door on the inside. Then he took out his revolver and placed it under his pillow. He told me to make certain that my gun was loaded and ready for use, and to put it where I could get my hand on it in an instant. He remarked that he had many men that not even he could trust when war was on.

We lay down on the Chinese stone bed close together. I then started a quiet conversation, saying that further war was foolish, as Mongolia already had independence, and that China would be of no use to the Mongols even if they should take it. He agreed that Mongolia had nothing to gain by warring with China, unless the Mongols again wished to rule over China. He said it was futile to conquer the country really as the Mongols did not wish to live in such a filthy, unhealthy place. I pressed this point hard by reminding him of numerous Mongols whom we both knew who had gone to China, either to attend festivities at the Manchu court or in attendance on the Dalai Lama, and died there.

I asked him why he did not stop the war. He answered that it was very difficult to stop a war once it had started. He said that he had no guarantee that the Chinese army would not break into Mongolia if the Mongols stopped the war.

I told him that Yuan Shih-Kai, the President of China, had promised me that whatever peace terms I agreed upon in consultation with the Mongols would be kept. I assured him that the Chinese army would be withdrawn and China cease interference in Mongolia. I offered to pay all the expenses of the rank and file of the Mongolian army back to their own homes, and to give Prince Na fifty thousand dollars to cover the damage the Chinese army had done in Mongolia.

I also told him that Yuan Shih-Kai was eager to have a strong personal guard and that he desired to employ any Mongol with a company of two hundred whom I recommended.

He was quite pleased with the idea of acting as guard to the President of China. It tickled his sense of humor to think that he should protect the chief of the very government he was now fighting. He said he would choose his two hundred men and come, if I would go with him to Peking. I finally got the conversation back to the matter of peace.

Sometime after midnight, the Prince agreed to talk things over with the other Mongol princes and try to persuade them to join in the proposal of peace. He said, however, that he would accept the Peking offer and go independently if none of the others wished to come or if they decided to carry the war on without him.

In the morning he gave me breakfast and sent two of his men back with me to my place at Tabo-Ol so that I should have them as messengers if I wanted to communicate with him. He promised to let me know later what day I could expect to welcome him at Tabo-Ol.

After several days he sent me word that the other leaders in the war would not agree to the peace terms, but that he had instructed his own men to desist fighting against the Chinese; he was ready to send all but two hundred back to his state in the Northeast, and to go to Peking with a bodyguard of two hundred for the President of China.

I went out to meet Prince Na and his men, and we greeted each other just north of my ranch. They came home with me. I had had a number of sheep killed and gave them a big Mongolian feast, serving to the officers fat sheep tails on brass platters, the same dish they had served to me.

The Chinese army was quite near. I did not want to have any trouble break out at my place between the two armies now so close together, so I sent one of my servants over to the Chinese general, whom I had found a very friendly man previously, and asked him to come and be introduced to Prince Na. The Chinese general was rather nervous, but he came to my tent at Tabo-Ol, and I called the Prince in to meet him. The general was pleased and surprised to find that the Mongol prince spoke excellent Mandarin, and they were soon drinking tea and chatting together in a friendly manner about the old days in Peking.

In the meantime I asked the Mongol soldiers to tie up their rifles in bundles and place them on oxcarts which I had ready for the purpose. I did not want the Mongols to have their rifles in their hands during the night, but promised them that the carts would be safely guarded until morning and that on the way to Kalgan they would actually have their rifles in sight the whole way.

Between Tabo-Ol and Kalgan a Chinese army of four thousand men were camped. I asked my friendly Chinese general from the near-by camp to go to the army commanders in this region and tell them that we would not ride through their camp, but that any of them who wished to meet the Mongol prince could do so at a certain place on the road where we passed. This the Chinese managed very well. With fine, quick courtesy they prepared a reception for us when we should pass the road at the place nearest their camp.

They had a large tent pitched to furnish cool shade. The Chinese commanders with a small escort were there, and received us in polite Chinese fashion. They served us with tea and good Chinese cakes. After conversation and refreshment we again proceeded on our march.

I had had two hundred sheep placed at different stages along the road to Kalgan, so every evening I was able to give the Mongols a good mutton feast. Before we reached Kalgan, scouts came out to tell me that the native Chinese were rather nervous about the Prince Na and his soldiers entering the city. I sent them back with my personal guarantee that there was no danger, and that the Mongols would make no trouble, but were entering as peaceful friends. The Governor of Kalgan met us outside the city gate, greeted us with Chinese politeness, and asked us to ride to his residence and drink tea with him. We went there and rested for a little while, and then proceeded to the railway station, to which the Chinese Government had sent special cars ready for me to use for the Mongol men and their horses. As soon as we had all boarded the train it left for Peking. At the station in Peking we were met by representatives of Yuan Shih-Kai, who had sufficient motor cars to take the Prince and me and all his men to the old Manchu palace which had been made ready as their residence.

The Chinese Government lived up fully to my arrangement with Prince Na, and he and his men served faithfully as the bodyguard of the President for many years. They were a notable feature of Peking life — tall, sun-bronzed, and stalwart, and always in attendance on Yuan Shih-Kai, no matter whether his star of popularity with the Chinese was in the ascendant or on the wane.

Prince Na had been the leader of the war on the border, but his departure did not end it entirely. Some of the wilder young nobles left behind drove off about four hundred of my horses and my herdsmen in revenge because I had taken away their leader. I at once wired to the Living Buddha, who was their Emperor, and he wired down to the Mongol army that these horses must be returned to me at once. If any one of my horses was missing from a herd it should be replaced by two good horses. The result was that in three days my lost herdsmen and horses were brought safely back.

The Living Buddha, Emperor of Mongolia, desired to live on friendly terms both with Russia and with China so long as the peoples of those countries did not interfere with Mongolian independence. The Mongol Government was running smoothly. The seasons since its formation had been good and the herds had thriven, so there was an abundance of the necessities of life far above what the people needed which could be bartered with the peoples of the neighboring countries for their products. The Buddha was akin to the Mongols in a love of festivities and gayety, so there were continual archery contests, wrestling matches, horse races, and picnics of all sorts throughout the country.

In the second year of the Buddha's reign I was asked to go to Peking for five years as Mongolian representative and as adviser on Mongolian affairs to Yuan Shih-Kai, then President of the young Chinese Republic. I finally went, but I did not find it possible to be of any real use as an adviser, as even when the things I advised were approved they were never carried out by the Chinese.

On November 5, 1913, Russia and China made an agreement between themselves in which Russia repudiated her promise to the Mongol Emperor to uphold Mongolian independence and promised China to use her power in Mongolia to provide for the autonomy of Outer Mongolia under the suzerainty of China. Then Russia and China both invited Mongolia to attend a tripartite conference at Kiakhta.

Finally the Buddha was persuaded to say he would send representatives to this conference, and asked me to go.

As both Russia and China were determined that I should not be included in the Mongol delegation, I returned from my appointment at Peking to life at my horse ranch on the plateau, glad to exchange the foul air of the city for the clean air of life in the open and the society of men for the society of horses.

The Chinese Government treated me with the utmost courtesy and diplomatic fairness. They not only paid me in full for the two years I stayed in Peking, but gave me an honorary medal of decoration and a cheque for thirty-six thousand taels the day I left. This cheque was the exact amount of salary I should have received for the three remaining years of the five-year term that I was supposed to serve.

Between September 9, 1914, the day on which the Mongols, through their spokesman the Living Buddha, acting as Emperor, agreed to meet Russia and China in a tripartite conference at Kiakhta, and June 6, 1915, the day of treaty signature, there was evolved a three-signature treaty which was of the nature and which produced the results that any history student expects when two nations that have a complex civilization and are parties to a secret agreement meet with a nation unaccustomed to work with written words.

Few Mongol princes ever succeeded in reading the treaty. After its signature life went on the same as before on the plateau, with the added confidence that both China and Russia had now "ex-

changed snuff bottles of friendship with Mongolia."
A Chinese dignitary with a bodyguard resided in a
residence provided for them by Mongolian hospitality, and no Mongol worried about the mere matter
of providing the residence or gave much thought
to the bodyguard except to remark that the representatives of the Chinese Republic dressed very
poorly and drably.

Russia did not attract attention to her power as
inscribed in the treaty, because she was occupied
first with war in Europe and then with the Russian
Revolution. Internal affairs kept China busy, and
she had no energy left for attempting to claim what
she had succeeded in having assigned to her on paper. Yuan Shih-Kai's party failed to make him
Emperor, and he died. Then with the strong man
gone from Peking, war bubbled up all over the
country.

In the spring of 1919 the President of the Mongol
Council of Ministers, Sain-noin Khan, died suddenly,
and the Chinese in Mongolia, in an attempt to
weaken Mongolia by setting laymen and priests
against each other, spread a rumor that he had been
poisoned by lamas. Then a little later a Russian
named Attamen Semenoff, with a group of rowdy
soldier adventurers, made overtures to the Mongol
Government for employment. Mongolia did not
want this man and his followers in the country, and
therefore rebuffed them. But at the conference of
lamas and princes met to discuss Semenoff, the
princes voiced their grievance in the matter of the
freedom from taxation enjoyed by priests. The

Emperor rejected the princes' request for equal treatment, and there was a hangover of bad feeling.

The Chinese seized this opportunity and secured permission to send General Hsu Shu-Tseng up to Urga. By the autumn of the year he had his entire army with him. Then Little Hsu set about making himself master in Mongolia.

Little Hsu's coup was so abrupt that the Mongols were caught unprepared. By force of arms he seized princes who had come to his residence as guests, arrested the Living Buddha and Badma Dardji (President of the Council of Ministers), and set soldiers in the office of Tsereng Dorch'i, Minister of Foreign Affairs. To prevent a bloody slaughter the Mongols signed the paper he wished signed — while other Mongols rode through their country gathering help and asked Russia to redeem her pledge of friendship.

The Mongols did not know that Russia had divided into two camps of Red and White. Some of the princes came to a Russian army commanded by Baron Ungern-Sternberg, and he returned with them and helped them punish Little Hsu.

Then eighteen months later the help that had been asked from Moscow came, and these Russians astonished the Mongols by starting a bitter war against the Russians who had arrived earlier. The Reds made an end of the Whites as cruelly as the Whites had murdered all the Jews they found in Urga after they had punished Little Hsu.

When this private war was finished the Soviets

exerted themselves to gain the confidence of the Mongols. They assured the Mongols of support for an independent Mongolia and for the preservation of the prerogatives of the Living Buddha, at the same time insinuating themselves at the elbow of all possible Mongol officials in Urga. China, alarmed, protested to Moscow, reminding Russia of their mutual pledges of friendship and agreement to share in Mongolia.

Four months after the entry of the Soviets into Urga a treaty was signed by a Mongol representative of the Urga government with the Russians giving Russia first right to trade in Mongolia. In December the Chinese traders were ordered to leave.

The Russians flattered and humbugged the Mongols who accepted them as advisers. They made it easy for the Mongols to borrow large sums of money and encouraged them to spend it in childish ways — one enormous loan was used for gold leaf to make the roof of a building glitter in the sun.

The noblemen who had clustered around the Living Buddha mostly returned to their own states, except the few who stayed in Urga out of loyalty to him. We could all see that he was seriously ill and had not long to live. As the Buddha sank into a state of semicoma, responsibility and power were tactfully taken from his hands by energetic Russians. Mongol friends who remonstrated died with invariable suddenness. The Buddha went to his final sleep on May 20, 1924, and immediately following his death the First Assembly of a new parliament met. They adopted a constitution founded on the Soviet pattern, and proclaimed Urga and the surrounding territory an independent republic without a president.

I maintained a residence in Urga, and spent a part of each year there, until after the death of the Buddha, but by that time practically all of my friends had gone elsewhere.

Many Mongol princes, especially the rulers of Inner Mongolia, have remained haughtily independent of any advisership, and have grown more bitter against Russian entry into the plateau with every year, so that now in 1929 there are many states which are unsafe for any Russian to enter on any errand. But in the territory of Urga the influence of the Russians has grown so strong since 1924 that they have become virtually dictators. Through the centuries in Mongolia men and women have ridden freely over the plateau on visits or errands, but the Russian advisers have drawn a cord around the territory in which they have power, and exercise a strict passport oversight. Every attempt is made to keep news from coming out concerning conditions, so that at this time Outer Mongolia has no communication with the rest of the world except through Soviet channels. The Russian advisers in North Mongolia have multiplied regulations and restrictions in a land which has been singularly free of complicated government rules. Only the future can disclose of what value the imposition of a complicated system of government on Mongolia will be.

In the beginning the young Mongols were pleased with the flattery of the Russians, but in the past year there has been continual evidence that the friendship is not so warm as previously. Young Mongols have been encouraged to go to school in Russia, and several have gone, but recently a group refused to stop at Moscow and independently went on to Berlin.

There is a constant rumble of rumor that the young Mongols do not think the prosperity under their Russian advisers compares with the prosperity of the days of their fathers, when less time was given to office details and more to the management of the herds. There have been several violent outbursts of insurrection in different places where the Russian hand has carelessly let itself be felt too heavily.

Very curiously, a tribe of Mongols, known as the Buriats, who lived in peace and prosperity under the pre-Revolution régime in Russia, are riding back into the plateau. They have little to say except, "We do not find life comfortable abroad any more, so we have come home." They are entering by the thousands, and are received in every independent prince's state upon payment of the same tax on herds that any Mongol who transfers his abode from one state to another would have to pay.

While Russia continues to hold first place in North Mongolia, the Nationalist Government of China is bidding for favor among the princes of Inner Mongolia, and has begun to make protests to Moscow against the encroachments of Russia on Mongolia.

Hemmed in between these two great countries, Mongolia has remained Mongolia for centuries, and to-day is stronger than she may appear.

IX

BUSINESS

BUSINESS in Mongolia is peculiar to the land and to the temperament of the people. The Mongols are not a race of traders and cannot be dealt with in the same manner as people who enter naturally and eagerly into business. Big business can be done successfully in Mongolia, but the trader must be possessed of the tact of the diplomat and be of a character which makes him akin to the people of the plateau and able to understand conditions there. The Mongol does not seek commercial dealings, but he is quite interested and ready to do business if approached in the right way. A thorough knowledge of the language and a wide Mongolian friendship are the first requisites of success.

During the thirty-five years that I have been in Mongolia, many foreign firms have expended millions in an attempt to start business, but have lost their money and closed down.

The Russians and the Chinese have been the most successful. The early Russian tea traders did extremely well; they built up great fortunes. For many hundreds of years the caravan route through Mongolia was the only tea route overland to Europe, and the Mongol camel puller was the only man capable of transporting freight successfully across the Gobi. Thousands and thousands of camels went from

Kalgan to Urga loaded with tea for reshipment by
cart to Siberia. Camels and oxen from all over
Mongolia were engaged in this trade, which was a
thriving business when I first came to live in the
country.

The Russian tea traders dealt carefully with the
Mongol nobles across whose states they desired to
travel. They made gifts to the princes — not exceedingly valuable gifts, but presents chosen with
careful attention to what a Mongol prince would
like from the Western world. And they treated the
people who freighted for them thoughtfully and
generously. In Kalgan, in Urga, and in all the trade
stations along the way, big kitchens were provided
as well as warm sleeping quarters for the men when
they came in. At these trade stations the Mongols
were the guests of the Russians. They could stay
as long as they liked, and were served with all the
food and drink they could consume.

The Mongols, accustomed to welcoming into their
own yurtas any traveler needing food or rest, appreciated this courtesy and did not presume upon it.
They conducted themselves in the trade stations exactly as they would have done in any Mongol encampment through which they passed when traveling.

This courtesy on the part of the Russians, together
with fair pay for the conveyance of freight, created a
good feeling. The Mongols were very willing, and
did their work well. They looked upon the Russian
tea agents as real friends, and brought them many
valuable presents. A genial, friendly atmosphere
characterized the trade up to the time when the

Manchurian Trans-Siberian railway brought it to
an end by opening a quicker and more economical
tea route.

The Russian tea traders were a fine type of men.
The trade was a business centuries old, in which
fathers passed their experience down to their sons.
There was garnered much wisdom through the years.
The Mongols trusted the young man who came out,
because they had known his father and grandfather;
and the young man knew how to deal with the Mongols, because his father also knew their fathers.

The Mongol likes tea, and he appreciated the
necessity for the Russian to import tea from China,
since it did not grow in Russia. The job of conveying
it across the Gobi was a courtesy which any friendly
people might undertake for another. The packing of
camels and oxen and the management of a caravan
across the plateau were work similar to what the
Mongol had done all his life.

Not all Russian businesses have succeeded so well.
The Russian Asiatic Bank sent out men and opened
offices in many places in North Mongolia about
twenty years ago. They were unable to do business
and had to close down. The Mongols were not interested in banks and did not consider them a
necessity. They had put their money into horses for
ages past, and had done very well. They had no
desire to keep fewer horses and possess instead a
paper book which said they each had so much wealth.
Possession to the Mongol is a material, tangible
thing. He holds a position in his community in proportion to the size of his horse herd, and has a feeling

of self-satisfaction in the possession of living animals. The Mongols looked with distrust on this attempt to bring a new set of values into their lives. The bankers were self-invited guests. The Mongols ignored them.

About this same time the Moscow Export Company sent an expedition into North Mongolia to discover the trade needs of the Mongols. They found the Mongols' lives bare of almost every article of European necessity, so they sent out scores of salesmen with tons of goods. Eventually the salesmen and their goods returned home again.

Russian and French prospectors visited North Mongolia and found rich deposits of gold. On the strength of their reports the Mongol-Ore Mining Company, with a capital of three million gold rubles, was founded. Baron Von Grote got the concession from the Empress Dowager of China by making her a small present of perhaps fifty thousand gold rubles in value. I worked with this concern from 1900 to 1902.

Machinery, such as has been successfully used in other parts of the world for gold mining, was sent from Europe at heavy expense. We expected to dredge sand, but when we delved a little below the surface we found we had to tackle stone and boulders, so more machinery had to come out from Europe at more expense. The workers were not skilled in the use of these machines, and we had to abandon them and resort to digging the gold out of the earth with pick and shovel and cleaning it by hand.

There was plenty of gold in the locality. The Mongols looked on interestedly at the work, but did not coöperate in it. Digging great quantities of gold out of the earth did not appeal to the Mongol as a profitable way in which to spend his days.

Laborers had to be imported. We got some Russians, but most of our workers were Chinese coolies who came from Shantung. They traveled in groups of six or seven, with one wheelbarrow between them which carried their food and clothes. We were not provided with funds to import laborers, so could give them nothing for the expenses incurred or the time taken on their journey. The Mongols refused hospitality to traveling Chinese, and they had to sleep in the open and prepare their own food as best they could. Often they were eight or ten weeks en route.

The summer was short. The greater portion of the year the earth was frozen too solid for mining, even if there had been no blizzards — and the blizzards of North Mongolia are terrible. Laborers had to be housed through the long winter, and even then hundreds died because of the cold.

Considerable gold was mined, but after it was mined there still remained the problem of transportation. A multiplicity of difficulties thwarted transportation. Eventually the Mongol-Ore Mining Company abandoned the work.

There are rich deposits of gold in other parts of Mongolia still untouched, as well as rich stores of silver, zinc, tin, iron, and copper. The Mongols have no interest in them and do not favor any activity which lessens the amount of pasture land, although if they were diplomatically handled a concession to mine could be arranged. But a mining project would have to be managed in a manner different from any so far undertaken.

Russian fur-trading concerns carried on by men of the character of the Russian tea traders did a good business up to the time of the Russian Revolution. Mongolia is a sparsely populated land with a cold climate. Fur-bearing animals thrive here in much greater numbers than the Mongols have need of. If properly approached, the people are quite willing to enter upon an export trade in furs.

The *tarbagan*, or marmot, a little animal which lives in a hole in the ground and multiplies very rapidly, is abundant in North Mongolia, Northeastern Mongolia, and Northwestern Mongolia. The marmot is not difficult to catch. The Mongol hunter camps out in the plateau in a little tent. The marmot is a very inquisitive animal, and as soon as he sees or hears anything strange he sits up on his hind legs and peers around. The Mongol hunter, knowing this, carries a banner of red cloth, which he waves in the air while he crawls close enough to kill his prey.

Mongols also use dogs to catch marmots. A well-trained dog brings home many animals every day. The dog watches until the marmot leaves his hole; then he takes up a position that blocks the marmot's avenue of return. When the marmot is caught in this way, with the dog between him and his hole, he rises up on his hind legs to fight the dog, who kills him with one snap of the teeth on his backbone, just below the head.

The Mongol hunter and his dog make an even division of the spoils. The flesh goes to the dog and

the fur to the hunter, who rough-cures the skin.
The Mongol does not value the fur very highly, but
there is a large demand for it in foreign markets.
Its value has increased a hundred per cent since I
first went to Mongolia.

Millions of skins are exported annually, and yet
the supply seems undiminished. Pelts in the market
are known as the autumn and spring marmot. In
the autumn, before the marmot goes down into his
burrow to sleep, he is very fat and his coat is thick
and fine; in the spring, when he first comes out, the
pelt is still nice enough to use, but not so valuable
as when first he went into his underground home.

Foxes are very common all over Mongolia, and
the fox fur here is of very fine quality. The red fox
is the most plentiful, but there is a goodly supply of
silver foxes, black foxes, and white foxes. The Mongol
treasures the silver fox most highly.

The fox is caught in various ways. One method is
by poisoning. The poison is generally put in a little
fat, the fat inserted in a piece of fresh meat, and the
meat thrown out on the hillside. Then next day the
Mongol rides through the territory in which he has
laid poison and picks up any foxes that have been
foolish enough to eat it. Dogs are also used for hunting foxes. A good dog will catch two or three foxes
a day. The hunter goes along on horseback and
assists in the chase, but the dogs do the killing. In
occasional cases traps and guns are used.

The Mongol prizes fox fur for coat linings and
sleeping rugs. There is also a large demand for fox
furs to export. The fox is plentiful, and so far there

is no danger of its being exterminated. Riding through the country one passes many foxes in a day. The fox makes his home in a rocky place if there is one available in the locality; if there is no rocky ledge, he digs a hole in the ground and uses this as a shelter in which to rear the young. Fox fur is good only in autumn and winter. In the late winter the fur gets rubbed off at the haunches from the animal sitting so much, and the pelt is less valuable. In the spring the hair moults, and during the summer the fox's coat is very thin.

Wolves are plentiful in Mongolia, and the Mongol wages continual war against them. The Mongolian wolf feeds well on animals from the domestic herds, on young antelopes, on hares, and even takes his toll of rats and mice. And he has a thick, healthy coat.

Mongols make use of wolfskins, but do not treasure them so very highly, perhaps because they have such an intense dislike of the wolf. The pelts are very good, and much in demand for export trade. They have multiplied many times in value since I went to Mongolia. The wolf is lassoed, trapped, poisoned, shot with a bow and arrow or the gun — in fact, killed in every possible way the Mongols can think of. The winter pelt only is good for use.

The Mongols have a superstition that if they kill a litter of young by digging them out or smoking them to death the mother and father wolf will track to his yurta the man who has done this unsporting deed and there kill one or more of his children in revenge.

Wolves in Mongolia are not generally seen in big

packs. Usually they run two or three together; in the mating season, five or six. Twice during the winter, in North Mongolia, I have counted packs of more than twenty. Once a pack of about ten took it into their heads to chase my motor car. This was in the winter. It was very cold, but there was little snow. I wanted to go quickly from Kalgan to Urga, so drove in my car. The wolves came valiantly after me. I slowed up until they got very near; then I stopped quickly and killed one and wounded another with my revolver. They made off as fast as they could, and did not show up again.

Squirrels are plentiful and their furs are of good thick quality. Thousands of skins are exported every year and millions more are used by the Mongols, yet the squirrel seems to continue as plentiful as ever. Lynxes, stone martens, badgers, and wildcats are also hunted for their pelts. Ermine and sable are found. Both come from somewhat similar members of the weasel family, which live in the forest, and both are difficult to catch. Ermine is white only in winter — a trick of nature's which protects the animal by turning its coat the color of the snow on the ground. Mongolian sable is soft, light in weight, and rich in color. Both sable and ermine are coveted by the Mongols and are seldom exported.

The pre-Revolution Russian fur traders went out of business with the Revolution, so they are no longer in the market. Many other European and American firms have sent scouts all over Mongolia and, observing the abundance of furs, plunged into the trade. One after another, throughout my thirty-five years, they have failed and had to close down because of their lack of understanding of the disposition of the Mongol, their inability to use the language, and their ignorance concerning climate and political conditions.

Numerous concerns, both large and small, have made attempts to do business in Mongolia. Two with the largest capital investment were the English concerns, Kaufmann and Company and the International Export Company. The former invested heavily in North Mongolia a few years ago, but they got very little out of it except trouble, and closed down with a debit balance. The International Export Company, who do very well in China preparing meat and eggs and other products in their factories for Western consumption, made preparations to deal in sheep in Southern Mongolia. They too had to close down after a few years.

In barter and trade with the Mongols, the Chinese have been the most successful of any race so far. The Chinese merchant has infinite patience. The managers of big wholesale houses send traders out into Mongolia with a pack of goods and a blue cloth tent, and wait a year or two for return on goods. The Chinese merchant puts up his tent near the encampment of a Mongol family, below a lamassery, or not far from the yamen of a prince. He makes himself known in a courteous way to the people near whom he camps, and does not push his goods upon them, but diplomatically lets them see that he has things which they might find useful. He is a peddler carrying bright cloth of silk and cotton, embroidery

thread, beads, food basins, long Mongolian pipes
fashioned with an artistic stem to tempt the pur-
chaser, tobacco pouches filled with tobacco which
he recommends as soothing after a hard day in the
saddle, millet, and flour. He studies the character of
the Mongol and brings only such goods as he is fairly
certain he can create a market for.

The Chinese merchant knows that the Mongol
does not have money, and he is quite content to take
animals and their by-products in payment for his
goods. Animals are plentiful, and so he gets a goodly
number for a small article. The Mongol does not
quibble over the price of any article he desires. Mongol men and women do not bargain. There is good
profit in the business for the patient Chinese merchant. If he makes himself well liked he finds a
welcome in every encampment. News of a man's
character spreads rapidly in Mongolia, and little
things make or break success in business here. The
trader gathers his produce at intervals and sends it
down by camel caravan or in driven herds to his
head office in China.

In North Mongolia now the Soviet Government of
Russia have entered into coöperative business with
the young Mongols. It is still too early to predict
how they will succeed. They have established a wool
trust, a transport company, and a system of traveling
merchants similar to the Chinese. Coöperation with
the Mongols has in it the germ of success.

Communication and transportation are important
factors in trade. Sometime before 1900, a Danish

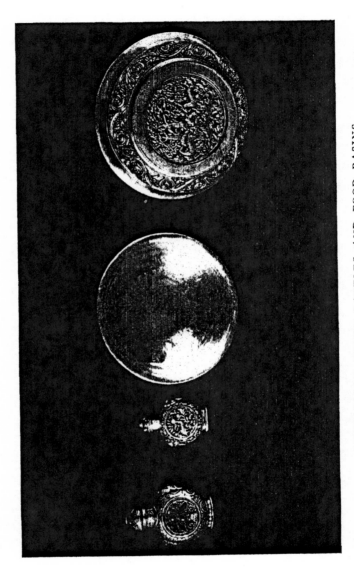

MONGOLIAN SNUFF BOTTLES AND FOOD BASINS

engineer, Sheirn, surveyed the shortest route from Kalgan to Kiakhta via Urga and built a telegraph line which connects China with Europe. By this line one can send messages across Mongolia, but the Mongols have not encouraged the building of branch lines.

This telegraph line is an everlasting wonder to the Mongol people. They fail to understand the importance of it, and argue that there is little need to send messages so quickly. It has been difficult to teach them to leave the telegraph poles alone. Often in the past the Mongols have used the poles and the wires for things which seemed to them more important than telegraphy. The wire they find especially good to tie around water troughs and fasten things generally, and the poles extremely handy to split up and light fires with. Except for the telegraph line there is no way to send messages in Mongolia but by couriers riding horse or camel.

Nowadays, therefore, the man in foreign business may receive an order for so many hundred pounds of camel wool by cable or telegraph in a few hours' time from his home office; but he must take into consideration the fact that it will take days or weeks or perhaps months for orders to go out to the Mongols to bring in the camel wool. Then, after the order has been received on the Mongolian plain, there is the matter of transporting the goods to be taken into consideration.

In the late 1890's, Herbert Hoover, now the President of the United States, then a young engineer, came up to look over the country and investigate the possibilities of railway construction. He stayed for two or three weeks and made a survey for the railway connecting the Mongolian border with the Chinese capital. The Chinese Government did not give Mr. Hoover's company this concession, but used the data which he collected and built a road themselves.

Since its construction this line has always been badly managed, because of the political turmoil in China. Yet it has paid well. The passenger cars are always crowded when the trains leave Kalgan. There is always a terrific scramble for place, and a goodly number of passengers who do not secure even standing room and have to wait for the next train. The condition concerning freight is the same; the amount of produce held at the station for transportation is always two or three times greater than the capacity of the freight cars.

There are no railways at all on the Mongolian plateau. In 1903, after I left the Mongol-Ore Company, I joined two Swedish engineers in making for the Russian Government a railway survey from Verkhne-Udinsk over the Gobi to the borders of China. But the Russians did not succeed in getting the permission to build this railway, as the Mongols did not see the need for it.

Even before his coronation as Emperor, the Living Buddha had more influence in Mongolia than any other person. He had a forward-looking mind and a keen interest in modern inventions. I took him one of the first Ford motor cars, and he was very pleased with it. After that he used his influence to secure the use of motor trucks in transportation over Mongolia.

During his reign as Emperor there were no taxes on the use of motors, and no special monopolies were permitted. Any and every one could use a motor truck. It is not necessary to make roads on the Mongolian plateau; a car can go almost anywhere.

At that time Russia and China were both too occupied with internal politics to give much thought to Mongolia. All of us in foreign business then who used motor trucks flourished, because we could send our goods so easily and quickly to either the Russian, the Chinese, the American, or the European market. But during the last four or five years the various Chinese governments have been so pressed for money that they have resorted to every possible means of gathering in a penny. Under conditions in China which have made the life of all governments short, the officials have been concerned in pocketing all the private revenues they can. So exorbitant taxes have been put on all goods from Mongolia, and no motor cars or trucks, except those of a favored Chinese monopoly, have been permitted to go beyond the Wall or to carry goods back.

This shortsighted Chinese policy keeps produce badly needed by war-ravished Chinese from going down from the plateau, where there is an abundant supply which goes to waste every year. It is to be hoped that the government now established at Nanking will follow a more sanely economic policy. Soviet Russia encourages Mongol trade, and so produce is being turned north to Russia.

The ox and the camel are the transportation standbys, as they have been for centuries in Mongolia.

Camel caravans are made up of groups of ten or eleven camels tied together with loose strings and led by a camel puller. Altogether there may be a thousand or more camels in a caravan.

Caravans cannot be hurried. The Mongol takes his own time. Centuries of experience have taught him how much a camel can successfully do, and he will not push his animals beyond their endurance. Camel caravans can penetrate to every nook and corner of Mongolia, bringing out valuable products for export. The Mongol camel puller will guide his caravan straight across the plain to any desired destination and there pack his loads and take good care of them, but often he will be a year, or two or three years, bringing in the goods.

I once had a caravan which came in with all my merchandise for export four years after I had expected it. Wool, furs, and so forth, were all in good order. An inventory tallied exactly with my book-keeper's lists. It is impossible to do business in Mongolia and get a quick return on one's capital.

Oxen caravans are even slower than camel caravans. Oxen are sometimes packed with produce in the same manner as the camels, but more often they are hitched singly in heavy wooden carts. These carts are hewn from tree logs, and the wheels are fastened to the axle, so that when the cart moves the axle turns with each revolution of the wheel. Oxen in caravan are driven along in single file in a string of forty to a hundred — sometimes even a thousand.

No food is carried for animals in Mongolia. Even

the beasts in caravans must forage for their own dinner. The animals have to be turned loose from the pack for a part of every twenty-four hours.

The camel is a quick feeder and not fastidious concerning what it eats, and quickly makes a meal on whatever green thing happens to be near at hand. The oxen are fussy feeders. They do not graze in sturdy progression, but hunt for tender, succulent grass. The camel caravan can go straight across country. The oxen caravan often has to make detours in search of good pasture.

Neither the traveler nor his goods are ever interfered with in Mongolia. The common law concerning this is written deep in the heart of the Mongol people. But when the traveler and his goods come to the borders of China and Russia this law no longer holds; bad men of both countries lie in wait to prey upon him.

Once when I pastured my herds and flocks about ninety miles from the Chinese border a band of rough-looking Chinese pitched eighty tents within three miles of my camp site. They had no animals with them, and so I feared that they were of evil purpose.

Two days after the coming of the Chinese I sat in front of my tent cleaning my guns ready for a wolf hunt, when a Mongolian camel caravan approached me at a run. It came to a stop in front of my encampment and the men unloaded their packs. I asked their business. They said that their camel loads were silver dollars en route from China to the Russian Asiatic Bank at Urga. They told me that a little way down the road they had met two armed men who demanded their silver, and when they had refused to give it up the robbers had laughed and said, "We will bring our companions and take it from you."

Soon after this twelve rough-looking Chinese men, armed with modern rifles, rode up close to the camel packs and dismounted. They walked boldly over to the silver boxes. Two of them lifted a box from the ground and they all speculated as to its value. While the Chinese were examining the silver boxes I took my guns and went quietly into a horse corral which was surrounded by heavy mud walls. Then I sent one of my Mongol companions out to ask the robbers what they wanted in my place. The Chinese leader sent back word that he had not come to molest me, but simply to take away the silver which the Mongols had brought there. I replied that by the common law of Mongolia this place on which my tents were pitched and my horses grazed belonged for the time being to me, and as it was my home I should defend it. I told my Mongol to tell the Chinese that I was not concerned with whether they were good men or bad, and that Mongolia was a big country and I would not interfere with their business in other parts.

A back-and-forth discussion went on for some time between the Chinese and me. They evidently decided that the caravan could not stay at my place forever, but would have to go on in a few days' time, when it could be robbed without interference. So they quickly mounted their horses and rode off.

As soon as it was dark my Mongol friends and I led the caravan across a mountain through secret passes where there was no road, and in that way the silver was saved.

Another time when I traveled from Mongolia to Kiakhta in company with Mongol friends we were molested in the forest where we camped for the night. We went to sleep with our rifles close beside us. I woke shortly after I fell asleep and accidentally put my hand up in the darkness and touched a gun barrel. I fastened my fingers on it tightly, pointed the gun skyward, and jumped up still holding the barrel. I found a villainous-looking fellow at the other end of the gun, but as he was not so strong as I, I was able to shake him off. The Mongols dealt with others of the bandit party and then we saddled and rode away in the night, as we decided it was not safe to sleep near the Russian border.

I could supplement these stories of treachery on the border with innumerable others from my own experience and from that of my Mongol friends.

The Mongols are staunchly honest. Except on the border, where they are of mixed blood and have lost their hereditary integrity, one can trust a Mongol with any amount. If a Mongol does take things on credit and defaults in payment later, by the Mongol common law his relatives and neighbors have to make up his deficits to the foreign creditor.

The Mongols have horses, cattle, sheep, wool, horsehair, hides, skins, and furs in sufficient abundance to be willing to trade them; but they are not interested in money, and prefer to barter their possessions for other tangible things. I am continually asked for the heavy silk which the pre-Revolution Russians brought into Mongolia, for waterproof blankets like those I use, for American cowboy saddles in replica of my own, for cloth like the material of my blue greatcoat, which is the stuff worn by the Danish Navy, and innumerable other things.

Business in Mongolia, if done all the year round, has to be on credit, as the products the Mongols have to barter are ready only in the spring and the autumn.

An ancient Mongol custom forbids the selling of milk. It must be freely given to a hungry traveler, but the common law forbids its sale, because it is the most valuable food the Mongols possess. There is nothing which can be purchased with milk that is considered of greater value than milk.

The Russians and Germans in various parts of Mongolia have attempted to increase the milk production, as they were interested in exporting butter and cheese. The Mongol has to be diplomatically persuaded to use good grazing land for cows so that they will produce more milk than he needs for his own food.

Despite these handicaps, good business can be done in Mongolia. I have exported more than two hundred thousand horses, and a proportionate quantity of wool and furs. The Russians are doing exceedingly well. The Chinese have done big business, and will do it again as soon as conditions permit them an equal opportunity with Russian merchants.

The Nanking Government has survived and

appears to be settling into the saddle. This government is made up of an intelligent group of men who will most certainly do away with the unfair restrictions against their fellow countrymen on the Mongolian border — the exorbitant taxes, and the unfair motor monopoly which turns northward into Russia trade which would otherwise go south to China. A free or low-taxed trade between Mongolia and China would make for prosperity in the North China provinces.

X

CHRISTIAN MISSIONS

The first mention of Christianity in Mongolia is contained in mythological tales written down in Europe, early in the twelfth century, of a Christian emperor who ruled Inner Asia and who was known as Prester John, or Presbyter Johannes. But nothing except myths have come down to us concerning this man or his kingdom.

The book of Marco Polo tells that Kublai Khan asked for Catholic priests to be sent from Rome to instruct the Mongols but that it was difficult just then to find priests to send. When two priests were finally appointed to go they got only as far as Persia. In 1307, when Temur, grandson of Kublai Khan, had succeeded to the throne, the Franciscan, John of Monte Corvino, reached Cambaluc, the Mongolian capital. He was followed by other Catholic priests, who traveled extensively over the plateau.

No permanent Catholic missions, however, were established in Mongolia until seventy-three years ago. Then a mission was founded at Jehol, the summer capital of the Manchu court. This was followed six years later by the opening of a mission at Soei-Yuen, and in 1868 work was begun at Si-wan-tze. These three stations are in territory cultivated by the Chinese, but from them the priests go out to work among the Mongols.

In 1817 the London Missionary Society planted a mission among the Mongol tribe known as the Buriats, at a place called Selenginsk, which lies to the southeast of Lake Baikal and near the boundary of Siberia and Mongolia. Reverend E. Stallybrass, Reverend W. Swann, and Reverend R. Yuille came out from England to found this work and carried it on with the help of their wives. The mission was established on Russian territory, and the Russian Emperor assigned a grant of land to the mission and gave seven thousand rubles for the erection of mission buildings. From this centre the missionaries went out on long preaching and teaching tours among the Buriat Mongols.

These missionaries made a translation of the Old Testament into the Mongol language, and it was printed in 1840 in Siberia by Russian imperial license. But before they had made much progress with the translation of the New Testament an order came from St. Petersburg commanding them to leave the country, and they had to return to England, leaving behind them the graves of Mr. Yuille, Mrs. Yuille, and their two children, and of the two wives and one child of Mr. Stallybrass. These lonely graves mark the site of the mission to-day. From England the survivors of the mission continued to correspond with friendly Buriats. They completed the translation of the New Testament, printed it in England, and shipped several hundred copies out for distribution among the Mongols.

I have several times found copies of the Bible in the translation of these Selenginsk missionaries in

Mongol tents pitched at various places on the plateau, the book sharing the sacred place on the family altar with the holy books of Buddhist faith from Tibet.

The London Missionary Society's next attempt to Christianize the Mongols was made in 1870, when James Gilmour was appointed to go from Peking into Mongolia. Leaving Peking on August 5, he traveled on foot with a Russian guide and reached Kiakhta, on the Siberian border, at the end of September. He visited the site of the abandoned mission near Lake Baikal, and then journeyed south again to Kalgan. From here he made several eastward excursions, and in November 1871, fifteen months after he left, he reëntered Peking. During his tour he had stayed with Mongols and worked hard at the study of the spoken and written language, preparing himself to preach and to write Christian tracts.

In April 1872 he set out on a second tour. This time he traveled one thousand miles through the northeastern portion of Mongolia. Following this trip he began to urge his mission to send him a colleague for the work in Mongolia.

That winter he lived at the Yellow Temple in Peking, where the Mongols who visited the Chinese capital congregated. He continued to study the language, and took up the study of the elementary treatment of sickness with Dr. Dudgeon. Again the next summer he went on foot to the Mongolian plateau.

In the winter of 1874 he married Miss Prankard, and she went with him to work among the Mongols in the succeeding summers, but in 1882 she was in such frail health that he took her home to England. While in England he wrote a book entitled *Among the Mongols*, and in making his reports of ten years of self-denial among the Mongols he said that not one Mongol had as yet been led to the Christian faith!

In 1884 he returned to the plateau, and at the end of that year a Mongol named Borjinto made a confession of faith and was baptized. The following year Gilmour's wife died and in his loneliness he threw himself with zeal into his work. He continued to ask for help from his home board. Twice missionaries were appointed and then had to go elsewhere; but finally Mr. Parker was sent. Mr. Gilmour died shortly afterwards, in 1891, and Mr. Parker carried on his work.

The writings of James Gilmour interested people of many nationalities and turned the thoughts of many missionary groups to the matter of Christianizing the Mongols. The work appealed particularly to the Scandinavian people, and some time after the publication of Gilmour's book, *Among the Mongols*, the Scandinavian people resident in the United States founded the Christian Missionary Alliance Society of New York. They sent to Scandinavia asking for volunteers to go to Mongolia. I listened to a minister in Sweden speak concerning Mongolia and volunteered to go, and twenty-six other young men and women came out from Sweden to work in China and Mongolia at the same time. This was in 1893. In an earlier chapter I have explained how I went to live in the state of Ordos and then went from Ordos to Urga.

From Urga I decided to journey across Mongolia to Kalgan. I secured a place in a camel caravan and was sixty days on the road. During these sixty days I had a most interesting time, and was treated with kind hospitality by all the Mongols as I passed through their country.

In Kalgan I stayed at the American Board Mission. There I met Miss Mary Rodgers of Albany, New York, a young member of the Christian Missionary Alliance Mission who had come to Kalgan for the summer. We were married two years later, and established a simple little home in Kalgan, where my wife continued her missionary work among the Chinese and from which I went out to work among the Mongols. We coöperated in the making of a Mongol-Swedish-English dictionary. Many people came to visit us, among our guests being Herbert Hoover, Sven Hedin, and others who have since become world-famous.

In 1899 Mr. C. W. Campbell, C.M.G., came up from the British Legation at Peking. He and I arranged to go together the next summer on an expedition into Mongolia. Early in the spring of 1900 I got the camels together ready for our expedition, and a group of Mongol friends came down from the plateau to escort us.

My wife and two daughters, Mary and Katherine, the latter only six weeks old, were to spend the summer in Hara-osa, on the Mongolian plateau, where I had arranged a summer home for them. Just a few days before I expected Mr. Campbell, serious anti-foreign feeling broke out among the Chinese.

Mr. Campbell was detained in Peking, and assisted very ably in the siege of that city. When the Chinese, who had been nicknamed "Boxers," began shouting "Kill the foreigners!" through the streets of Kalgan I decided to get away from there with my wife and the small children. I was glad then of the camel caravan and provisions I had made ready for my planned excursion with Mr. Campbell.

The families of three other missionaries joined us, and we went out to Hara-osa. There we made camp and waited for the other missionaries at North China to join us.

I led this company of seventeen grown-ups and six children across the Mongolian plateau to Urga. Three of the missionaries who joined us at Hara-osa had been attacked and wounded before they could get away. We made them as comfortable as we could. Our caravan was a curious one: three Chinese oxcarts with mats put on top to keep off the burning sun; the camel cart, which I made as comfortable as I could for my wife and her two babies; and we men on camels and horses.

The Mongols along the way were as a rule good to us, but it was a long and tedious journey. After thirty-six days we arrived in Urga. There I heard that all the property of the mission with which I was connected had been destroyed, as well as our books and the dictionary over which my wife and I had worked so hard for several years.

The rest of our party went back to their homes via

Siberia. I was troubled by the need of money, and did not like to apply to my mission for it now that all the mission's property had been destroyed. So I joined the Mongol-Ore Company as I have explained.

Life was primitive at the Mongol-Ore Company mines, and my family suffered from the hardships there, so when I had earned enough money to be able to do so I took them to my wife's home in America. I then returned and worked on the survey of a railway across Mongolia.

After this I sent for my family and joined the British and Foreign Bible Society. I established my family in Kalgan for the winter months, and built a summer home for them at the horse ranch I had started at Tabo-Ol. I crossed and recrossed Mongolia in every direction distributing Bibles for the Society. My caravan consisted of ten camels, packed with Bibles, and five riding ponies, as mounts for myself and my helpers. I lived as the people of Mongolia lived. I entered into their sports, and I was drawn into their affairs as I traveled from state to state. I liked the people and they liked me. The Living Buddha was exceedingly friendly to me and interested in my books. When I stopped in an encampment folk traveled many miles to visit me. I worked at putting the Bible into easily understood language in collaboration with Anton Almblad. Men, women, and children listened attentively when I read to them from my Bible, and they bought many thousands of copies to read themselves or keep until a traveler passed who could read.

So the years passed until 1913. I had made innumerable friends and given them the Christian Bible. I then resigned, and suggested to the British and Foreign Bible Society that Mr. Almblad should be given my place. He is still engaged in this work, and is stationed at Kalgan.

Shortly before 1900 the Scandinavian Mission of Chicago opened work among the Mongols west of Pao-tow. The missionaries had just begun to be able to use the language when all of their number except Mr. N. J. Friedstrom were slaughtered by the Boxers. He had to flee. A year later he opened work at Patse-bolon on the north side of the Yellow River. Other missionaries came to join him, and they established an extensive work. The mission has supported itself from its foundation by its farms, which are irrigated from the Yellow River. These are model farms, where the tillage of the soil and the care of cattle by modern scientific methods are demonstrated to both Chinese and Mongols. The mission also runs schools for Chinese and for Mongols.

The Swedish-Mongolian Mission opened work among the Mongols north of Kalgan soon after 1900, and they now have three mission stations and nine missionaries working in Inner Mongolia. Dr. Erickson is located at Hat-um-sum, and does an extensive medical work throughout the surrounding country. His mission station is always surrounded by a cluster of tents set up by Mongols who have come from far and wide for medical treatment. The Prince of Durbit has made Mr. Erickson his special medical attendant, and he is also frequently called to the palace of the Prince of Sunit. Dr. Ollen is stationed at Gulltjagan, and does an equally extensive work in his locality. Both doctors have Ford motor cars. Unfortunately these cars have been used for a good many years and are now in a decrepit condition, so the doctors both have to waste a great deal of time in keeping them in repair. Both machines should be replaced with new cars by people interested in the mission's medical work. The medical work is more than these two men can do, and they should be relieved of all such unnecessary toil as mending broken cars.

Doctors practising in the Western world can scarcely realize the multitude of things that these two doctors are called upon to do in a single day. They are the only foreign doctors in Mongolia, and their work includes everything from the treatment of fevers and such illnesses to the performing of major operations. They both have reputations which have spread through the length and breadth of Mongolia. Their work attracts to their missions hundreds of Mongols who through physical healing become interested in the Christian faith.

In addition to their medical work, the three mission centres of the Swedish-Mongolian Mission all conduct schools, run churches, and do an extensive evangelistic work throughout the country.

The Pentecostal Mission has conducted work in Mongolia from their headquarters at Chang-peh for a number of years.

There are a number of centres of work in addition to the missions already mentioned in this chapter.

The most successful of these is the mission founded a few years ago by a young Swedish girl, Miss Hulda Wiklund. Miss Wiklund has been extremely popular with the Mongols, nobles and commoners, since she first came to the plateau. She is an excellent horsewoman, which appeals to the Mongols, and is possessed of a fearless straightforwardness that wins their admiration.

Miss Wiklund founded her home at Na-men-ol in 1926, and a colony of Mongols have pitched their tents around her. She has had marvelous success in the treatment of the sick, and the story of her skill in curing illness has spread so that people are brought to her from great distances.

Her method of teaching is by example in her own daily life. She has founded a school for Mongol children in which the teaching is done by Mongol teachers whom she has trained since she came to the plateau seven years ago. She has recently built a church, as the attendance at her Christian services has grown too large for a yurta or her own living room.

But despite all the mission work which has been done on the plateau, there are a very few Christian converts. The Mongols do not easily give up the way they have followed through the centuries.

XI

EXPEDITIONS

DURING my years in Mongolia I have been privileged to count as my friends, and to accompany on their expeditions, many scholars who have come to the plateau to delve into the historic past of this land.

It was in 1899 that Mr. C. W. Campbell spent a month with me in Chahar. We planned an expedition into East Mongolia for the summer of 1900, but the Boxer trouble prevented our setting out on the expedition until 1902. In the spring of that year mule carts brought his luggage from Peking to Kalgan and over the rim of the plateau to a Mongol encampment at Hara-osa, where I awaited him with a caravan of pack camels and riding horses.

Mr. Campbell was accompanied by Chabeh Singh, a surveyor, lent to the expedition by the Indian Intelligence Department. We first made a survey of Angul Nor, the largest sheet of water in Chahar, measuring the greatest width of the heart-shaped lake as seven miles and the average depth as four and a half feet. The water of this lake tastes strongly of soda, and we found no fish in it; but the cattle and horses of the district thrive on it, and the camels love it.

Our caravan drank of the water with no ill result, but when we sent a sample to Shanghai to the health officer the report was: "Highly poisonous as a beverage, and destructive to animal and most vegetable life."

We next visited the remains of the two ancient walled cities, Khara-balgar and Chagan-balgar. The latter is supposed to be the Chagan Nor of Marco Polo's book. Then we went on to a deserted walled city called Kurta-balgar, where we camped on June 24, and from there journeyed to Hui-tsung Ssu (the Temple of the Gathering of the Clans), which is graphically described by Gerbillon, an eyewitness, as the scene of the meeting of the Khalha princes with the Manchu Emperor K'ang Hsi and the signing of the treaty of 1691. And from there we went to the Monastery of Shou-yin Ssu (Good Cause Temple), which was built with a donation of one hundred thousand ounces of silver from K'ang Hsi's son.

After this we marched to the ruins of Chagan-hota, which folklore names as one of Kublai Khan's imperial residences. These walls enclose a space three hundred and fifty yards square. The northwest wall, which is intact, is twenty feet high. It is built of two facings of stone set in mortar packed with earth, and tapers from fifteen feet wide at the base to five at the top. There are evidences of three great doorways and two open pavilions.

We camped for two days on the shore of Dalai Nor and went carefully over the territory described by Gerbillon in his remarkable journey with Father Pereira and the Chinese ambassadors who were sent to Nertchinsk to conclude the first Chinese treaty with Russia in 1689. He mentions royal ruins, but as Prjevalski, who circled Dalai Nor in 1871, did not

mention them, we supposed that weather had ob-
literated them in the intervening centuries and did
not really expect to find any traces of them. So we
were agreeably surprised to learn from the Mongols
with whom we camped that there was a *balgar* a
couple of miles away.

We found a rectangle of walls nine hundred yards
from north to south and eight hundred yards from
east to west. A part of the wall is twenty feet high
and thirty feet broad at the base. The walls are of
sandy loam. They are now a succession of longitu-
dinal mounds. In the middle of the northern half of
the ruins we traced one large hall eighty feet square,
and to the rear of it a rectangular room fifty-five
feet by forty-five feet, formed of fifteen carved plinths
of white marble, much damaged, on which pillars
could have rested.

In the front of the ruins, to the south, we found
two black stone lions, and more to the south two
massive stone turtles, near which were two monu-
ments of white marble with inscriptions of the Yuan
dynasty, the name by which the Mongols ruled
China. We found here pieces of royal-blue tiles
identical with those found in the Kurta-balgar ruins.

A Chinese book, *Meng-ku Yu Mu Chi* ("Records
of the Mongols"), has a passage which clearly refers
to this place. This book says that Kublai authorized
it to be built in 1271, and that his grandson Temur
came here to live when he left China and died here
in 1368.

While camped on the shore of Dalai Nor we made
a casual survey of the lake, which is sixteen miles

from northeast to southwest and ten miles from east to west. The water has a soda flavor, is greenish and clear, and contains an abundance of fish. In the reeds on the south shore are many water birds — geese, ducks of several species, sheldrakes, teal, plover, lapwing, redshanks, snippets, gulls, and terns. The whole district is the nesting place of birds — larks, martins, swallows, sparrows, magpies, pipits, chats, and peregrines, as well as ravens, kites, buzzards, and fishing eagles.

We moved our caravan along the west shore of the lake and turned northward on lovely thick greensward, sprinkled with magenta clover and yellow vetch, which rose in gentle undulations. Mr. Campbell was astonished by the antelope herds that we passed continually, as one always does in crossing the pasture lands of Mongolia. He used to stand and count all in sight — often more than five hundred.

We journeyed about four days north-northeast out of the Abagha district into Jun Hochid, past the Shilin Gol, a clear stream of twenty yards in width which waters this part of the plateau, to a nameless ruin near Lama Sume; then through the Lama Sume Valley, where wild rhubarb and licorice abound, on to the river called Churm Gol, which has its source in the Khingan Mountains.

We halted for a night at the summer encampment of the Prince of Jun Hochid. Next day the Prince appointed one of his men as our guide. This guide led us on a straight course to the Khalha River, and on the morning of July 26 we pitched our camp beside the river near a limestone bluff named Krei Ul.

From this bluff we could see the silver thread of the river as it wound northwestward between sand banks, its course bordered by a thicket of willow, hawthorn, elm, and currant bushes, while away from the thicket on either side stretched emerald-green pastures. The east pasture ascends to hills we measured to be one thousand feet above the river bed.

We followed the south bank of the Khalha River for four days, then crossed it at the embouchure below Lake Bur, where it splits into channels. The broader channel is a hundred and twenty yards wide. Both are shallow, measuring three feet at the deepest place. From west to south Lake Bur extends further than the eye can see, and the strong wind then blowing lashed it into a thunderous sea. We bought turbot and an eight-pound carp from some Mongol fishermen and had a good fish dinner.

Then we went into the Barhut territory and on to Ulan Nor, the long narrow lagoon renowned for its pastures, where in 1698 Gerbillon spent a week in the suite of the Manchu High Commissioner who held the first Council with the Khalha princes. This region is called Bur Dalai (Coupled Oceans) by the Mongols. On August 5 we reached the Kerulen at a point five miles southwest of the Altan Emul (Golden Saddle), a pair of brown hills famous in Mongol legend, through which the river flows.

After traveling along the Kerulen until August 20 we came to the ruins of Para-hota, the earth walls of which are now grass-grown mounds which make a rectangle of sixteen hundred by fourteen hundred yards. Outside the earth wall we found the remains of what appeared to have been a moat. Three hundred yards from the centre of the west wall there is a pyramid forty feet high built of bricks, and two hundred yards from the centre of the south wall there is another pyramid. Both are in a crumbling condition, but still standing, although Gerbillon remarks upon them as half ruins when he passed in 1698. Near the south wall there is a large mound of building débris, — rubblestones, broken bricks, and fragments of marble, — but we found no blue tiles. This ruin is supposed to have been built by Toghon Timur in the middle of the fourteenth century.

In our journey down the Kerulen River we stopped at the royal encampments of the princes of San Pei Tze, Batur Jassak, Akhsa, Daichim, and at the palace of Tsetsen Khan, the most famous race-horse breeder in Mongolia. We left Tsetsen Khan on August 29 and made a direct course for Urga; on September 4 we crossed into the valley of the Tola River, and the next day reached Urga.

From Urga Mr. Campbell made excursions out to various places, including a trip to the oval tumulus on Mount Kentei, which I had visited earlier, and which is thought by some scholars to be the tomb of Genghis Khan, disputing sites in the northeast corner of Ordos and on Bogda-Ol for this distinction.

When I was adviser on Mongolian affairs to Yuan Shih-Kai, then President of China, Dr. J. S. Andersson of Stockholm was adviser on geological affairs to the Chinese Government. We were both resident in Peking in the winter, and one summer I invited him to spend the torrid season with me at Tabo-Ol.

He spent the entire summer collecting old bronzes. He dug up ancient coins, quaintly figured bronze mirrors, bronze hairpins, graceful-handled bronze knives, bronze bowls with pictures raised in relief all around their brims, and many other relics of the distant past. The story spread that my guest desired these things, which, as all Mongols knew, constantly work up through the green turf, and there was a continuous pilgrimage of black-eyed Mongol children to our camp fetching in bronzes they had picked up in play. The children came shyly to offer these trinkets that the grown-ups of their own tents had considered of no value, and scampered happily away to show the shining silver coins Dr. Andersson gave in return for dull bronze.

During his services as adviser to the Chinese Government, Dr. Andersson spent all of his holidays collecting porcelains and bronzes, first in China and then in Mongolia. Since the termination of his advisership he has given all his time to this work and from it has collected data which fill in many pages of ancient Mongolian history that were formerly blank.

He has traveled extensively in Southern and Western Mongolia, combing the ground in this territory for bronze and pottery relics of the past. His collection is housed in Stockholm — where it can be seen by all visitors — and is a most interesting assembly of implements used in the distant past. Dr. Andersson is still busily at work delving into the Mongolian past, penetrating into more territory every year in his effort to complete the history of the bronze age.

One of the first foreigners I met when I went to Urga for the first time was the Russian explorer, Mr. Koslov. Mr. Koslov came out to Mongolia when he was a very young man to work with the then aging Russian explorer, Prjevalski. Since Mr. Prjevalski's death he has worked alone. Neither winter blizzard nor summer sun ever stops his work in the investigation of everything which throws light on the lives of the very early Mongols.

Mr. Koslov is assisted ably by his wife, who catalogues and marks carefully all of his geographical, archæological, and zoölogical specimens. He has under him a staff of Russians and Mongols who are always kept busy. Mr. Koslov plans every detail of the work, so that no time is lost by any of his workers waiting for something to do.

His exploratory expeditions travel by camel. They are slow of movement, but he prefers the camel caravan because slow progress makes for thoroughness. He has been in Mongolia nearly half a century and has worked over large territories. He has done much valuable research in the old city of Karahata, where he has unearthed many valuable documents and fresh data concerning the ancient Mongolian capital.

When I saw Mr. Koslov last, about two years ago, he was still living in a Mongolian yurta in Urga just as he has always done. He lives frugally so that as much money as possible is free for his exploratory work. The weather was bitterly cold and blizzardy, and the country was covered with deep snow, so it was impossible to do any country work; but Mr.

Koslov and assistants were busy arranging the specimens collected during the open months of the past
year, getting them ready to send to the Moscow
Museum.

Neither in Russia nor in Mongolia has revolution
ever disturbed Mr. Koslov. He goes quietly on with
his work, seemingly oblivious of all the political hap-
penings of the world. His mind is completely absorbed in the work of ferreting out the Mongolian
past, and he has been undisturbed by any political
changes. He continues to send his specimens serenely
to the Moscow Museum under the Soviet régime
just as he did during the time of the Czar. His attitude is that history is too long to let oneself be upset
by the changes which happen in a man's lifetime.

I think it must have been in the summer of 1918,
or possibly 1919, when one of the most charming
men I have ever met, Roy Chapman Andrews, was
brought to my home in Urga by a mutual friend. He
is well known for the unusual research work which
he has done for the American Museum of Natural
History. When I met him in 1918 he had already led
expeditions into Alaska, Burma, China, and the
borders of Tibet. In the summer of 1918 he had come
with his wife into Mongolia to continue his historical
researches. His pretty young wife was the able
photographer of his expedition, and had wonderful
success with photographs on plates which pictured
scenes in their natural colors.

They crossed the Mongolian plateau from Kalgan
by motor cars, then discarded the cars and did their

work in the country on horseback, with a small caravan which carried equipment.

It is a joy to meet a scientist like Mr. Andrews, who not only does his scientific work thoroughly and well, but has an artist's appreciation of the beauties of this land which I love so dearly. In that first summer I was charmed with the enthusiasm he showed for the bluebells, the daisies, and the yellow roses which bloom so profusely in Mongolia, as well as for the fossilized bones of ancient life for which he was searching.

At this time Mr. Andrews planned a larger and more extensive exploration, and I agreed to accompany him on it. This expedition was called the Third Asiatic Expedition of the American Museum of Natural History. I was with the expedition for three months. My friend the Jalang-Se Lama, who was then Prime Minister of Mongolia, did much to facilitate this expedition for us. The Jalang-Se Lama made it possible for the expedition to photograph the lama temples and lama festivals, which had never before been photographed, as well as gave us introductions in the country in which Mr. Andrews desired to work.

The expeditions went out from Urga to the Altai Mountains. Near Chagan-Nor Mr. Andrews discovered the dinosaur eggs which aroused world interest and are now exhibited in the American Museum of Natural History.

Mr. Andrews had with him on this expedition, as on all his later trips, specialists in various lines, as he collects plant, animal, and geological specimens. The

most important work of his expeditions are the paleo-
logical researches. He has discovered fossils of un-
known animals of immense size which convince even a
layman that the prehistoric climatic conditions in
Mongolia must have been entirely different from
what they are to-day.

In the autumn of 1923, after I had been with the
Third Asiatic Expedition, I was surprised to receive
the following letter from the American Museum of
Natural History: —

> I have the honor to inform you that at a meeting of the Board
> of Trustees of the American Museum of Natural History, held
> on November 12, 1923, the following resolution was unani-
> mously adopted: —
>
> *Resolved,* That the Trustees desire to express their deep ap-
> preciation of the invaluable service rendered by Mr. Frans A.
> Larson in carrying out the plans of the Third Asiatic Expedition,
> and in recognition of his interest in the expedition's work take
> pleasure in hereby electing him an honorary *Life Member* of
> the American Museum of Natural History.

Mr. Andrews has made several later expeditions
into Inner Mongolia, during which I have been privileged to be with him for short times. In recent years
he inaugurated the use of motor cars for the conveyance of expedition workers, with a camel caravan to
carry oil and supplies. This has been a tremendous
help in the work. It makes it possible for the scientist,
when he hears of a locality where there are exposed
fossils, to go quickly to the place, and the motor
trucks are a convenience in transporting the fossils
across the Gobi down to the railway.

Mr. Andrews has written a book on each of his

expeditions, which those interested in Mongolia are well advised to read. He spent five months last year on the Mongolian plateau and unearthed fossils of greater size than have ever been found in Mongolia before. His expedition has made preparations to go out again this summer.

Perhaps it is because I am not an author that I find it impossible to write adequately of Sven Hedin, because there are no words with which I can tell of the perfect sympathy with which he entered into our nomad life on the plateau from the first hour of his arrival. Again and again I have heard the Mongols remark on this, so I know that I am not alone in feeling it.

I met Sven Hedin first in 1897. He had just returned from a hard journey through the Taklamakan Desert. He had lost his outfit and nearly lost his life. He was cheerful and cool about the whole experience — absolutely undaunted, but resolved to return again and conquer the desert. He believed that the secrets of ancient Mongolia were hidden under Taklamakan. We talked that first time of meeting of going there to work together one day, and twenty-nine years later we went.

Between 1897 and 1926, each time Dr. Hedin and I met we talked about this expedition. Once — about 1915, I think — we journeyed together from Kalgan to Urga, when he was en route to explore Northern Mongolia. In 1926 he came to me in Peking and said, "Did you really mean that you would go with me on one of my expeditions?"

I answered him quickly, "I should certainly be honored and pleased to go."

"Then it is settled," he answered. "Let 's get our caravans ready."

It took several months for us to get a caravan together, as we had to have three hundred camels and a year's food supply for sixty-five persons. This is the largest scientific expedition that has ever crossed Mongolia. The workers include Mongols, Chinese, Swedes, Germans, and Danes. We traveled from Kuei-hua-cheng to Taklamakan by the old caravan route across Mongolia, and were eighteen months on the way.

I left the expedition shortly after we reached Taklamakan, as I had to return to Inner Mongolia, but the scientists are still working there, and have explorations planned which will occupy them for many years to come.

We had twenty-six blue cloth Mongol tents with us. These are tents which can be put up by one man in ten minutes. Each has a centre ridgepole which rests on two uprights. The tent cloth is so cut that when a tent is pegged down there are angles facing in every direction. No matter how hard the wind blows, such a tent cannot be torn down; it does not flap and flutter like a foreign tent. This tent has been evolved through centuries by the Mongols. It is the tent used by the herdsmen.

A fire can be built in the tent and a corner lifted so as to make a draught which carries out all of the smoke. I slept in my tent all of eighteen months and did not have a fire even in the worst blizzard.

SVEN HEDIN AND FRANS LARSON

We erected our twenty-six tents every time we camped, so we made a little city every night. However, we did not all travel together all the time, as the different scientists had to cover different grounds in search of specimens of special interest. The lead caravan with the freight went on the main route, and little caravans of three or four tents branched off at times, to rejoin us later. The scientists studied the geographical, meteorological, and archæological aspects of the country as we traveled.

In winter, when we were about halfway to Taklamakan, heavy blizzards made travel difficult and our camels broke down from exhaustion. This happened in a stretch of land where no Mongols camp in winter. We had to unload the freight. All the party except two Mongols — Monka and Serrat — and I took the burden-free camels and went on to the nearest encampment.

We three were left with the freight, as it would have been unwise to leave it alone, possibly to be snowed under by the blizzard or to be picked up by wanderers. We piled the freight boxes up to form four walls and covered the top of our little house with camel saddle sticks and spread felt over them. Then we made a fireplace in the middle and spread camel blankets all around.

We used this hut to eat our meals in, but slept in our blue cloth tents. We each wrapped up in a thick black bearskin rug and were warm at night. We had to stay here three weeks, in which time we saw no one except ourselves. We had no water except melted snow. Wolves, wild asses, and big-horned sheep came close every day to look at us and discover what sort of beings we were.

I enjoyed this experience immensely, but was glad to see the caravan of fresh camels which eventually came to relieve us. We then joined the rest of the party and all went on toward Taklamakan.

This journey was a trip in which there was much real physical hardship. The Mongols and I were accustomed to this kind of travel and reveled in it, but we were agreeably surprised at the splendid spirit with which the Chinese and the Europeans met bad weather and kept cheerfully on.

Dr. Hedin was a marvel to all of us. At the end of the day's journey the rest of us were ready for food and sleep and threw ourselves down to rest as soon as camp was made. Sven Hedin never showed exhaustion even if he felt it. He worked until far into the night every night writing and drawing with his facile pencil.

As Serrat, one of our Mongols, commented one day: "He lives two lives to our one, because he does the same as we do every day, and every night makes pictures and writes books."

In addition to this he also planned every detail of the work of the expedition and did a large amount of scientific research himself, as well as correlating the work of all the others. Sven Hedin has written so beautifully of this trip, illustrating this as all his other books with such excellent pictures, that it is futile for me to attempt to do more than mention it here.

Dr. Hedin and his fellow workers have already

made some marvelous discoveries. The Chinese Government are very much interested in this expedition and have aided Dr. Hedin in every possible way. He has won the hearts of the Chinese, just as he has won the hearts of the Mongols.

I hope I have made it clear that this expedition is the largest ever undertaken in Asia and a direct continuation of the researches to which Dr. Hedin has given all his life since early youth.

XII

CLIMATE AND GEOGRAPHY

MONGOLIA is a plateau of one million, three hundred and seventy thousand square miles, slightly hollowed in the centre, and rises gradually from the southwest to the northeast. It is bounded on the north by the Siberian provinces of Tomsk, Yeniseisk, Irkutsk, and Transbaikalia, with the Altai and the Sayan Mountains rising from the steppes; on the east by Manchuria and the Khingan Mountains; on the south by China, with the Great Wall dividing the two regions already separated by nature; and on the west by Sinkiang, Dzungaria, and the Tien-shan.

In all seasons of the year Mongolia is brilliantly lit with golden sunshine — sunshine which warms the back even on a midwinter day in the same way as the sun does in Switzerland. The sky is a clear soft blue, and across it float thistledown clouds. The sunsets and sunrises are brilliant with color. The plain is not flat, but rolls like a billowing ocean. From any position the eye roams over an expanse of country that it would take several weeks' riding on galloping horses to cover; always there are hills, and still more remote hills, shading from the green of near pastures to the deep purple of the dim distances.

The air is crisp, fresh, and dry. Even in midsummer the nights are so cool that a man requires a blanket or rug in which to sleep. The winters are severe, despite the brilliant sunshine of the daylight hours; but no more severe than the winters of Montana, of Sweden, of Northern Germany, or of Scotland.

Mongolia is not a land for the people of the tropic races, but it is an excellent climate for folk from northern climates. I am always healthy in Mongolia.

In the northwest the plateau reaches its highest altitude and the land comes under the influence of the Siberian climate. The winters are savage, but summer fills the land with song, flushes the plateau with grass, and sprinkles it with flowers. The rolling country is covered with green grass and dotted with blue lakes. The lakes, teeming with fish, are surrounded by marshland in which many varieties of lovely-plumaged and sweet-voiced birds live.

The northern plateau is broken by ranges of snow-capped mountains, and in consequence summer rains are frequent and there is no lack of pasture. Here are forests of larch and spruce, luxuriant meadows, and a wealth of wild flowers. The saline pastures give an abundant grazing to flocks of sheep and herds of horses and humped camels. Beyond this there is a zone of comparatively barren steppes, leading up to alpine pasture and a world of rock and snow. In summer shepherds graze their flocks on the rich grass that grows in this high place.

This part of Mongolia covers an area of approximately three hundred and seventy thousand square miles. The chief mountains are the Russian Altai, on the northwest, the Sayans on the northeast, and the Ektag-Altai on the southwest, which form a border range facing the Dzungarian depressions; and the Kentei on the southwest, separating the higher terraces of Northern Mongolia from the lower Gobi.

The chief rivers are the Jabkan, Yenisei, Selenga, Orkhon, the Tola, and the Kerulen. These rivers all run north except the Kerulen, which runs east.

The chief lakes are the Ubsa, which is twelve hundred square miles in extent, the Kobdo, and the Kara-usu. The yearly rainfall in this district is about nine and a half inches; the temperature varies from about twenty degrees below zero, Fahrenheit, in January to sixty-four degrees above zero in July.

The Mongols do not build towns in the Western or Chinese sense of the word, but Urga, Uliassutai, and Kobdo are centres in this district where large numbers of Mongols pitch tents together and dwell for a part of every year; and in each of these centres there are a goodly number of temples, and mud houses, the latter built by Russian and Chinese traders.

South of this area lies the zone of Gobi. This occupies only about one quarter of the whole of Mongolia, but because it is the section most frequently crossed by people not native to Mongolia its characteristics have come to be noised abroad as those of the entire Mongolian plateau.

The motor route from Kalgan to Urga runs across Gobi. Several attempts have been made to make the motor-way go through more fertile country, but have so far all been thwarted. As late as last year

MR. LARSON SPENT THREE WEEKS OF MIDWINTER IN THIS
NO MAN'S LAND

a way was planned across the fertile pastures of the state of a certain prince in Mongolia. The Mongols made no comment during the days of survey; they kept silent while a motor inn was built for the accommodation of Chinese representatives of the motor line and traveling passengers; they maintained their silence the day the first cars drove halfway across the state and put up for the night at the convenient inn they had built.

The inn, the cars, the passengers, and the motor-line representatives disappeared in the night. In the morning only even squares of newly laid turf showed that the grass pastures had ever been scarred by outsiders. China still calls the princes of Inner Mongolia her vassals, but the motor cars attempted to run a new route only once.

The Chinese call the Gobi zone "Hau-hai," which means "Dry sea." This section, of arid desert nature, is a depression in the plateau. On the northern edge it averages about thirty-five hundred feet in altitude and has a stony surface on which coarse grass grows. In the south it descends to two thousand, four hundred feet and is at its lowest level. Here there are large tracts of sand. The surrounding ranges intercept the rainfall so that it is very light, but even the sandy area is not entirely barren; tufts of wiry grass, garlic, and shrubs are plentiful. Gobi is the breeding land for the two-humped Mongol camel. The area of the Gobi region is about four hundred and eighty thousand square miles, extending about a thousand miles from east to west, and varying from four hundred and fifty to six hundred miles from

north to south. It has no permanent rivers. The
northwest winds of winter discharge their moisture
on the Sayan slopes, and the southeast winds of
summer exhaust their humidity on the Khingan
heights.

Middle Mongolia — or Gobi — and Southern
Mongolia are almost treeless. Drying winds sweep
across this part of the plateau. Still, it is a curious
fact that anywhere in this area one has only to dig
twenty or thirty feet below the surface to come upon
ice-cold water; in many cases even in the Gobi water
has been found two yards under the surface of the
sand. This shows that there is an abundant supply
under the whole plateau, and it would be comparatively easy to plant stretches of forest right across this
section, which would break the strong wind and make
the ground more damp and fertile.

Although rains are scarce in summer, there are
some severe cloud-bursts. I am now visiting in this
section of Mongolia. It is the seventh day of July.
Two days ago I wrote this far in this chapter. It was
a hot, sultry day, so that I found it necessary to
close my white-felt yurta tightly to keep comfortably
cool. I was interrupted by the three elders of the
family whom I am visiting. They came to my yurta
and drew me into an argument which waxed between
them concerning the advisability of taking the herds
of sheep out to distant pasture, as the heat had
burned up all the grass near at hand.

The younger brother held out against taking the
animals from home. The uncle and the elder brother
favored sending them. The three wives also pressed

into my tent. They supported the younger brother. As we talked a high wind arose. The earth was powder-dry. Thick dust whirled in sandy clouds. Then the rain fell as though thrown from great dippers.

The entire family welcomed the storm with cries of delight. The children dropped their clothes and ran wildly into the storm. The uncle borrowed my field glasses, sprang on to one of the saddled horses at the hitching place, and cantered to the high hill where the obe stands. The brothers scudded out to shepherd the lambs into tents the women cleared. I helped corral the animals, and then joined the uncle on the hilltop.

I must have been on the obe hill about half an hour when I sighted a great cloud of dust a mile or two away from us. This dust ball swept on toward us at a terrific speed; it was so quick that one could not see what lay behind it. The dust cloud passed three or four hundred yards below our encampment. Behind the dust ran a raging torrent of water — a mighty swirling river which carried everything mercilessly before it. Luckily our tents were pitched well away from the path the water took.

This river surged by for several hours, and finally subsided about dusk. Next day we rode along the path of the mysterious river. The way was strewn with the bodies of men, women, and children, with thousands of sheep, cattle, and horses that had been hobbled or tied so that they could not run, with the tents and oxcarts and bodies of Chinese merchants, and was clotted with a sodden mass of felt yurtas with bright painted covers, embroidered shoes, and silver hair ornaments.

Nature, which had swept humanity and humanity's trappings so ruthlessly away, had already caused thick grass pasture starred with delicate flowers to spring forth under a few hours' sun. The flood disappeared as mysteriously as it came — for its source was no broken dam, but an opening of the heavens. To-day, the second from the cloud-burst, all the plain, which was a burnt-up sandy waste forty-eight hours ago, stretches away in a circle to the horizon richly mantled with green. The sheep feed contentedly. The cows gave full pails when brought in this evening. The children roll and frolic with pleasure in the soft turf, and joy in having plenty of milk to drink again. The Mongols depend upon nature sublimely; they never dam water against a drought; but if it were irrigated Gobi would be a fertile garden like the irrigated desert areas of the United States. Should the Mongols give the crowded Japanese an area here, they would make it bloom at all times.

Marching along the eastern side of Gobi is a zone about a hundred miles wide which is well watered, well wooded, and rich pastured. The Khingan Mountains shelter this fertile area. They shield it from the cruel winter winds which sweep across Gobi and force the summer winds blowing from the Pacific to feed it with gentle rain. Thus gracefully Mongolia drops to the border of Manchuria.

Between the Great Wall of China and the Gobi lies the area which the Chinese call "the land of high grass." This section well deserves this name. The climatic influence here is from the Pacific and there is grazing all the year. The snowfall is seldom too heavy for the animals to scrape down to the abundant grass, which is sweet and nourishing.

This district is almost barren of trees, although trees thrive when planted here. There are no brooks or springs of water which gush to the surface, but water is found everywhere by digging twenty or thirty feet into the ground. Wells usually give sparkling clear water icy cold on the hottest day, but in some districts the water is so strong with salt or with soda that it is impossible to use it even for making tea. In several places in this area are salt deposits from which the people of Mongolia have drawn salt as they needed it for centuries.

The Chinese have pushed out beyond the Great Wall in a fringe now nearly a hundred miles wide, and with poor tools and poor seed they produce rich harvests wherever they break soil in the "tall-grass country." Wild flax grows in abundance here, and the exiled Chinese use it to spin strong cloth to make clothes.

The Mongols, though they have moved back into Mongolia from the Wall, continue to have plenty of pasture, despite the land which the Chinese have put under the hoe.

That part of Mongolia which is called Ordos is separated from the rest of Mongolia by the Yellow River. It is an area of forty thousand square miles of undulating plateau south of this river. It is second to Gobi in aridness, but when rain falls luxuriant grass springs up through the sandy soil, the shrubs on which camels fatten put out a lusty growth, and the plateau is patterned with delicate pink eglantine, sturdy yellow buttercups, trailing blue morning-glories, lavender spikes of foxglove, and five-petaled white-stars.

CPSIA information can be obtained at www.ICGtesting.com
Printed in the USA
LVOW060201050512

280476LV00001B/93/A